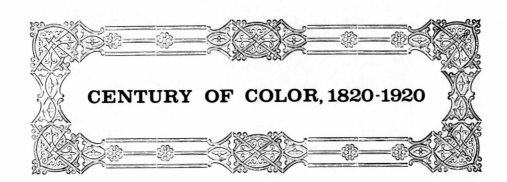

CENTURY OF COLOR, 1820-1920

House-Painting Guide

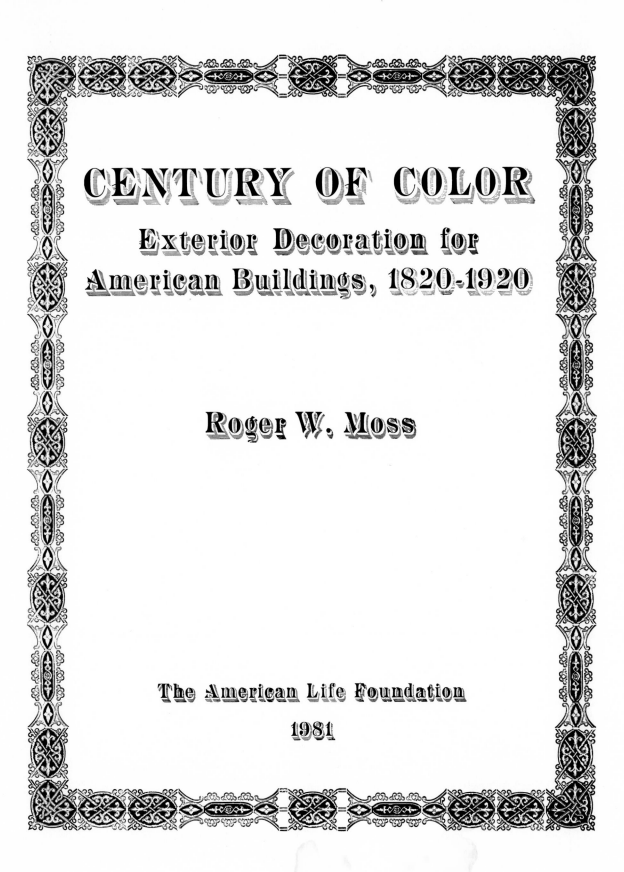

CENTURY OF COLOR

Exterior Decoration for
American Buildings, 1820-1920

Roger W. Moss

The American Life Foundation

1981

For
Elizabeth & Victoria
Comprendre c'est pardonner

First Edition

ISBN: 0-89257-051-2

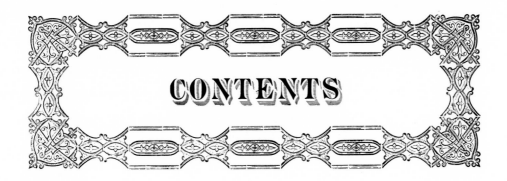

CONTENTS

Acknowledgments

DURING the past two years, I have travelled to nearly every part of the United States lecturing for The Victorian Society and *The Old-House Journal* on the topic of "Painting the Historic House, 1820–1920." I had been drafted to deliver these lectures because in 1976 The Athenaeum of Philadelphia reprinted a large, Victorian book on house painting to which was added a new introduction by Dr. Samuel J. Dornsife and an extensive bibliography drawn largely from our research collection of original paint sources. The project had been something of a joke in publishing circles. Not only was such a book technically difficult to produce because of its large format, color plates, and paint chips which had to be tipped into the binding by hand, but the high cost of the finished product made it commercially unpromising. However, within two years all 5,000 copies of *Exterior Decoration: Victorian Colors for Victorian Houses* had been sold. Since then there has been a brisk out-of-print market for the book at twice the original price.

Regardless of the success of *Exterior Decoration*, and the obvious demand for additional copies, the book had several flaws which kept The Athenaeum from issuing a second edition. It only contained twenty color plates, some of which were more picturesque than informative, it only illustrated colors for a limited range of styles and periods (1880s), and the high cost put it beyond the means of many home owners. *Century of Color* is not being published as a replacement, however; *Exterior Decoration* remains useful as a reprinted document, as does Dr. Dornsife's pioneering essay and bibliography. Rather, this book is aimed at that large audience which I have met and attempted to help over the past few years. It is based on a wide variety of original documents similar to *Exterior Decoration* and covers an entire century rather than a single decade. The plates are selected for the wealth of detail they contain and are arranged roughly by period and by building type. Finally, *Century of Color* is being issued in a less expensive format for wider distribution. It is immodestly hoped that this book will encourage the owners of American houses built in the last century to select colors that are historically proper for the age of the structure and to place those colors to emphasize correctly the rich character and detailing intended by the original builders. If readers seek here technical information on paint chemistry or detailed reports on the microanalysis of specific buildings, they will be disappointed. My intention is to provide a practical handbook for the old-house owner who asks, "What colors should I paint my house and how should they be applied?"

Several people deserve to be mentioned for their help in making this project possible: Samuel J. Dornsife, ASID, Williamsport, PA, for first introducing me to the topic; the trustees of the Ella West Freeman Foundation, New Orleans, LA, for supporting The Athenaeum's early work on exterior paint colors; Patricia and William Eldredge, Chris Wearsch, and Phillip Barress of The Sherwin-Williams Company, Cleveland, OH, for their assistance in the preparation of the manuscript and the development of the paint chips which appear at the back; John C. Freeman, Executive Director of The American Life Foundation, who conceived the project and has seen it through as publisher; and Frank S. Welsh, historic paint color specialist, Bryn Mawr, PA, for his aid in documenting the colors. In addition, I want to thank those people who have lectured with me over the past two years, particularly Clem Labine, publisher of *The Old-House Journal*, Gail Caskey Winkler, ASID, University of Wisconsin—Madison, and Hugh J. McCauley, AIA, Philadelphia, PA, who have contributed more than they realize to helping me shape what follows. At The Athenaeum of Philadelphia, my associates Eileen Magee, Sandra Tatman, Keith Kamm, and Ellen Batty, have each assisted in the development of the collections on which this book is based or in the preparation of the manuscript. Mr. George Vaux, President, and the Directors of The Athenaeum deserve special thanks for enlightened and uncommon encouragement. Finally, to all those brave owners of Victorian houses who have risked the outrage of their neighbors and battled with their spouses to repaint with proper colors, a special thanks. You have led the way where many now follow.

ROGER W. MOSS
January, 1981

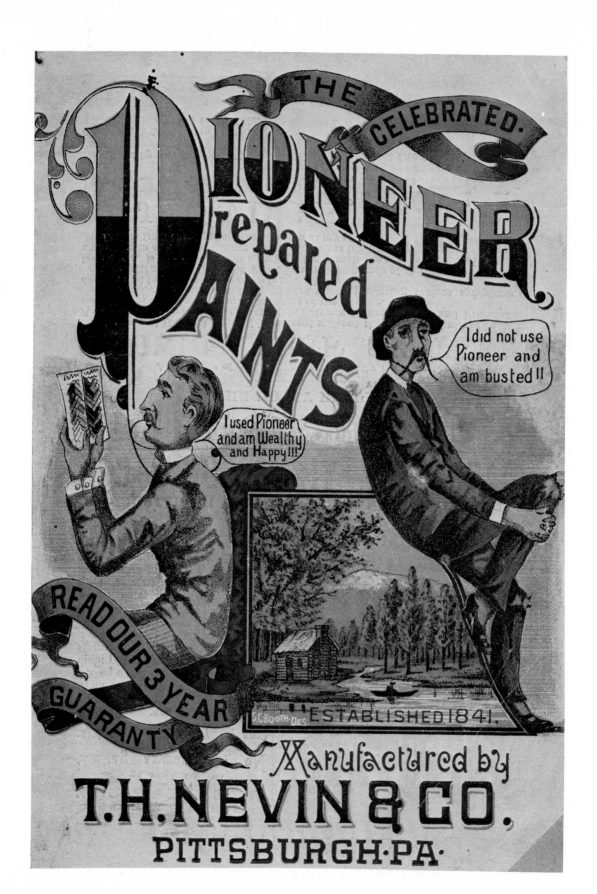

The Century of Color

IN THE WINTER OF 1842, the celebrated English novelist Charles Dickens traveled to America. He reached Worcester, Massachusetts, in early February. "All the buildings," he later wrote, "looked as if they had been painted that morning.... Every house is the whitest of white; every Venetian blind the greenest of the green." [1] That same year, the American architect Andrew Jackson Downing published his *Cottage Residences*; he, too, took note of houses painted white with green shutters: [2]

There is one colour ... frequently employed by house painters, which we feel bound to protest against most heartily, as entirely unsuitable, and in bad taste. This is white, *which is so universally applied to our wooden houses of every size and description. The glaring nature of this colour, when seen in contrast with the soft green foliage, renders it extremely unpleasant to an eye attuned to harmony of coloring, and nothing but its very great prevalence in the United States could render even men of some taste so heedless of its bad effect.... To render the effect still worse, our modern builders paint their venetian window shutters a bright green! A cool dark green would be in better taste, and more agreeable to the eye, both from the exterior and the interior.*

Not content to publish a plate of alternative colors (SEE PLATE 4), Downing continued his attack in the *Horticulturist* and in his influential *The Architecture of Country Houses* (New York, 1850). The exterior color of a house, he argued in the latter book "is of more importance than is usually supposed, since,

next to the form itself, the colour is the first impression which the eye receives in approaching it—and, in some cases, the colour makes its impression, even before we fully comprehend the form of the building." Downing felt that white was widely used because it was thought to be more durable and because it made a house appear new and fresh. Curiously, he fails to mention that white was also associated with those Greek and Roman architectural forms that so influenced the early years of the new American Republic, styles that were being called into question in the 1840s as more picturesque Gothic and Italianate Revival buildings made their appearance. Downing and other American Romantics thought buildings should be integrated with nature, not imposed upon it. The glaring purity and rationality of Classicism starkly declared man's separation from his environment; natural coloring, picturesque lines, and landscaping that softened the harshness of coursed masonry and sawn boards, helped to restore the balance between man and his surroundings. [3]

The criticisms that Downing advanced against white in *The Architecture of Country Houses* are several. First, "it is too glaring and conspicuous. We scarcely know anything more uncomfortable to the eye, than to approach the sunny side of a house in one of our brilliant midsummer days, when it revels in the fashionable purity of its colour. It is absolutely painful." Second, white "does not harmonize with the country, and thereby mars the effect of rural landscapes. Much of the beauty of landscapes depends on what painters call *breadth of tone*—which is caused by broad masses of colours that harmonize and blend agreeably together...." The alternative is to avoid colors not found in nature. "In buildings, we should copy those that [nature] offers chiefly to the eye—such as those of the soil, rocks, wood, and the bark of trees—the materials of which houses are built. These materials offer us the best and most natural study from which harmonious colours for the houses themselves should be taken." Not green, however, because "houses are

FIG. 1 *Advertisement for Pioneer Prepared Paints from the T. H. Nevin & Company* Annual Almanac *(Pittsburgh, 1886). Anticipating Madison Avenue writers of the twentieth century, Victorians blatantly suggested that the key to happiness and wealth was the use of one product over another. The prosperous gent on the left is contemplating a sample card of Pioneer Prepared Paints.*

not built of grass or leaves." Rather, buildings should be painted *"soft and quiet shades called neutral tints, such as fawn, drab, grey, brown, etc., and . . . all positive colours, such as white, yellow, red, blue, black, etc., should always be avoided. . . ."* In addition, the size and placement of a house should influence its color. *"In proportion as a house is exposed to view, let its hue be darker, and where it is much concealed by foliage, a very light shade of colour is to be preferred."* If a house is large, it *"may very properly receive a somewhat sober hue, expressive of dignity,"* but if the structure is a small cottage, it should be painted a lighter color, *"a cheerful and lively tint."* [4]

In the mid-nineteenth century, painters often mixed sand into the paint applied to cornices, window and door frames, and porch details to simulate stone. Downing suggested mixing the sand directly into the oil prior to its application with a brush. Gervase Wheeler wrote that *"sanding paint, or mixing sand therewith, besides assisting in its preservation, takes away from the oily glare and glisten of ordinary pigments, and by lessening the refracting power, gives to the surface of the building a softer and more pleasant tone of coloring."* The limited literature on this practice suggests that the sand was *blown* onto wet paint with a bellows more often than it was actually mixed. This latter practice is more usual in modern restorations where the base of the paint is oil.

Before leaving Downing, it would do well to examine his views on the second major problem of exterior painting: color placement. Once having adopted a color from the fawn, drab, grey, or brown scales, there is still a danger of monotony *"produced by using the same neutral tint for every part of the exterior."* [5]

Now there are features, such as window facings, blinds, cornices, etc., which confer the same kind of expression on a house that the eyes, eyebrows, lips, etc., of a face, do upon the human countenance. To paint the whole house plain drab, gives it very much the same dull and insipid effect that colourless features —(white hair, pale eye-brows, lips, etc.,) do the face. A certain sprightliness is therefore always bestowed on a dwelling in a neutral tint, by painting the bolder projecting features a different shade. The simplest practical rule that we can suggest for effecting this . . . is the following: Choose paint of some neutral tint that is quite satisfactory, and, if the tint is a light one, let the facings of the windows, cornices, etc., be painted several shades darker, of the same colour. The blinds may either be a darker shade than the facings, or else the darkest green. If, on the one hand, the tint chosen is a dark one, then let the window dressings, etc., be painted of a much lighter shade of the same colour.

By following Downing's rules, the owner of a Gothic or Italianate house would probably adopt a scheme of Downing Sand trimmed with Downing Stone and Downing Slate (Trim); or, Downing Straw and Downing Earth. Several such combinations are suggested by the affinity chart (SEE, PP. 99–103).

During the decade prior to the Civil War, a number of architectural critics restated Downing's views,

most notably Henry W. Cleaveland, William and Samuel Backus, Gervase Wheeler, M. Field, and Calvert Vaux. [6] Until more detailed studies of actual houses from the 1845–1860 period are published, we may only speculate on the extent to which the new coloration was adopted. Architect designed buildings from the late 1840s through the Civil War, especially in the Gothic and Italianate Revival styles, probably will reflect the new taste. Vernacular and traditional building in more or less Classical Revival styles probably will tend to follow the white-with-green-shutters color scheme. In an essay on "Art in House Painting," a writer for the Devoe Paint Company in the 1880s summarized the evolution this way: [7]

The change came very gradually, the white being at first tempered for the sake of variety with cold tints of grey, lavender, green [sic!], blue, and other colors, totally unfit for the purpose they were intended to serve, but still of value as stepping-stones to better things; the rare examples of the use of deeper shades, of warm rich tints and a variety of colors in exterior decoration, were falsely spoken of as 'loud,' when really, compared with the old style of painting, their effect was subdued and restful. The new idea in painting, as it was termed, had, however, found friends, it was permanently before the world, and gradually the sole consideration of utility became tempered with a desire for artistic effect.

Certainly by 1861, when John Riddell published the first American architectural pattern book with full-color plates, the Downing colors were much in evidence (SEE, PLATES 5–11). The palette he illustrates is still somewhat lighter than that presented on the late 1860s "Homestead Colors" sample card of the Devoe Paint Company (SEE, PLATE 12). This card is one of the earliest examples of American ready-mixed paint samples, and it is one of the few containing only the low saturated, muted colors associated with Downing and the other Romantic architects. [8]

The population of the United States doubled between 1860 and 1890—a raw statistic with dramatic influence on the building trades and the hundreds of companies that developed to supply the burgeoning market. A number of technological innovations in the post-Civil War decades influenced the color of American buildings. The paint industry developed both machinery to grind pigment in oil and containers in which this ready-mixed product could be shipped safely. The railroad network spanned the nation, and it allowed large and well capitalized manufacturers in urban centers such as New York, Philadelphia, and Chicago to reach distant markets. (Heretofore, homeowners were forced to depend on local painters who mixed dry colors with lead and oil for each job.) In addition, the development of inexpensive paper and high-speed presses encouraged colorful advertising brochures and architectural pattern books that reached thousands of Americans building houses.

It is commonly recognized by historians that the nineteenth-century transportation revolution and advanced printing technology helped to bind the nation

1776   1876

FIG. 2 *The Averill Chemical Paint Company was issued a patent for ready-mixed paint on July 16, 1867. On their advertising flyer of the 1870s, they illustrated a wretched colonial painter mixing dry colors and oil by hand and a happy "modern" artisan enjoying the benefits of their ready-mixed product. D. R. Averill's "patent" paint, however, was not popular because the pigments were improperly mixed and tended to sink in the can, causing the paint to streak when applied. This problem was not overcome until 1876 when Henry A. Sherwin invented a new paint grinding mill.*

FIG. 3 *Throughout the nineteenth century, painting specifications ordered that front doors and, occasionally, all exterior window frames, be grained to simulate hard woods. Normally this was executed by the painters with brushes, combs, and bits of rag. In the 1860s, however, the Devoe Paint Company patented a graining machine that was designed for use on large areas.*

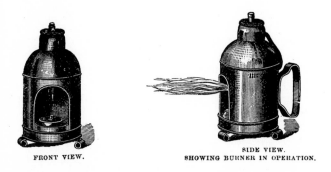

FRONT VIEW.   SIDE VIEW.
SHOWING BURNER IN OPERATION.

FIG. 4 *Restoration architects recommend that old paint never be burned off with a torch because of the danger from fire. The Victorians were not so careful. The above advertisement shows a mid-nineteenth-century blowtorch.*

together following the Civil War. To students of Victorian architecture as well, the availability of pattern books for building houses, such as E. C. Hussey's *Home Building . . . from New York to San Francisco* (New York, 1876; SEE, PLATES 35–40), and trade catalogues, supplying such diverse products as stoves, tile, millwork, and paint, helps to explain the homogenization of American building in the last decades of the nineteenth century.[9] By the 1880s, a house built in Central City, Colorado, or in Zanesville, Ohio, would probably share stylistic characteristics and would certainly be painted in the same color palette of greens, olives, grays, yellows, and browns—colors much darker and richer than those advocated by the pre-Civil War generation of architects.

To what extent American paint companies encouraged the use of the richer colors to create a market for their ready-mixed paints is a moot point. Certainly their advertisements encouraged the adoption of the new colors. The Wadsworth, Martinez & Longman Company stated: "The extensive distribution of Color Cards, Lithographs of Buildings in color, and many other methods placed before the public, to aid in making suitable selection of proper shades of color for painting, has provided the means to change from simple white with green blinds to the many pleasing shades of color now presented upon almost every residence."[10]

America did not automatically switch to the rich colors of the post-Civil War years with the arrival of the first train loaded with Lucas, Devoe, Seeley Brothers, or Sherwin-Williams ready-mixed paint. The "browning" of America was a gradual process which would itself be swept away at the turn of the century. Roughly speaking, there were four major color phases in the nineteenth century: late Federal through Neoclassical (c. 1820–1840); Gothic and Italianate Revival, or early Victorian (c. 1840–1870); late Victorian (c. 1870–1890); and Colonial Revival (1890–1920), which saw a return to Neoclassical detailing and a renewed interest in early American architecture. Although this is a gross over-simplification, these four periods have fairly definable color palettes ranging from a dominant white with green shutters, through the pale earth tones, to the dark, rich—if somewhat "muddy"—colors that most people associate with late Victorian buildings, to a gradual return to white and light pastels.

The introduction of richer, deeper colors in the 1870s is reflected in the Harrison Brothers "Town and Country" paint sample card of 1871 (SEE, PLATE 14). The lighter Downing colors survive (as they will throughout the century), but greens, oranges, and olives have begun to creep into the palette. Two movements encourage this change. First, the growing complexity of architecture as America moved from the historic revivals (Gothic, Italianate, and Mansardic) toward Queen Anne, Stick Style, Eastlake, and Shingle Style buildings. Second, there was a shift, encouraged by the Aesthetic Movement, toward an emphasis on materials, texture, mass, volume, and structure. Isaac H. Hobbs wrote in the second edition of *Hobbs' Architecture* (Philadelphia, 1876): "Designing a building is like a battle upon canvas of color, each part striving for supremacy.... Give each [element] its just due, and they will all be quiet; no wrangling; but one beautiful, peaceful, harmonious assemblage, all coming forward with their little gifts, giving them quietly and freely." [11] Two years later, Henry Hudson Holly specifically criticized Downing: [12]

Some years ago it was quite customary to paint houses a sort of dirty yellow, which custom arose from the fact that Mr. Downing, in giving some figurative instructions as to the color employed, said: 'Pluck from the ground the roots of the grass, and the color of the earth thereon will be the color of the house.' Now, the gist of this was that the color of the house should be in harmony with the landscape; but some of his unimaginative followers failed to see that it was not to be taken literally, and hence arose a fashion which, we are glad to see, has gone by, of painting houses an offensive mud color.

Holly, too, disliked white houses; white "is no color at all, always cold and glaring, and making an ugly spot in the landscape: we find nothing to warrant so forcible an intrusion." In cities, Americans should follow the example of the Middle East: "study their picturesque use of external colors, and let the walls of our cities assume new life and meaning by contrasting tints of various bricks, stones, and brilliant tiles." In the country, lighter tints might be used, but

I would not have it supposed that positive colors cannot be employed to advantage on the exteriors of country houses. For example, green as the color for the blinds not only has a cool and cheerful effect, but seems to be that chosen by Nature in which to clothe her natural bowers. Still, if neutral tints are used on the body of the house, green is apt to appear in too violent contrast unless a line of some other harmonizing color be interposed. If the general tone of the house is drab or olive, a line of Indian red between this and the blinds would produce a relief. But in coloring our houses it is certainly well to follow the architect's advice, since an improper application of paint might quite nullify the effect of his design, and render that ridiculous which was intended to be dignified; small, that which was to appear large; and obtrusive, that which was to appear modest and retiring. [13]

The movement toward ever richer colors which began in the 1870s continued into the 1880s. "The objections against employing white for outside purposes," stated the author of *Every Man His Own Painter* in 1873, "apply with equal force to other primary colors —they are all too conspicuous and formal in appearance. Yellow is the only one which can be tolerated, and even the shade of that must be carefully selected, or better left alone. Gray also is objectionable, being cold in appearance and especially inappropriate where green is present." [14] According to a writer for Devoe Paint Company in the 1880s, this new taste in exterior decoration developed together with the Queen Anne style.

In its embellished form it admits, without any appearance of incongruity, of the production of the quaintest effects both in the groupings of the parts of a building, the general appearance produced and the working out of the details in the shape of doors, windows, etc. It is, moreover, a form that admits of the most comfortable and attractive arrangement of the interior, and above all, and what most concerns us, it furnishes an opportunity for the greatest display of taste in coloring and exterior decoration. The many fronts, diversified as to material, with visible framing, shingle or smooth covering, the gables, the porches, etc., all provide a means for the employment of parti-colored effects, the most attractive and artistically valuable feature of modern house painting, and one that the old box-pattern house, with its plain flat front, does not so readily admit of. [15]

One need only examine the color plates in this book to see the relationship between increasing complexity of architecture and the richness of "parti-colored effects" (SEE, PLATES 37–60; ESPECIALLY, 55–60).

E. K. Rossiter and F. A. Wright, in their *Modern House Painting* (New York, 1883), cautioned against "picking out small members in a brighter color than the rest, in order to enliven the whole. This gives a building a choppy and mincing effect, and instead of bringing out and helping the architectural design in a subordinate way as color should, it is apt to result in undue emphasis of features which ought to be kept back, and to give other parts a relative importance that is far from desirable.... We refer more particularly to the custom of painting chamferings, mouldings and ornamentation in a positive color—frequently a bright red. These features in a design ought to be appreciated in light and shade only. They bring out the form in detail, and the emphasis of shadow is quite good enough without recourse to more violent methods."

In their book *Modern House Painting*, Rossiter and Wright stated that "the old puritanical hatred of color, which found its natural outcome in white houses with green blinds, has had to give way; at first, to a compromise, in which neutral and sickly drab tints played a prominent part and, later, to more advanced notions, in which the more positive colors find a chance of expression." The old rule of one body color and a darker trim color no longer applies. "The present style of architecture does not oblige its enforcement, but rather tempts to the use of more colors and a diversified treatment. Where the lines and surfaces are so much broken up as they are now, the old ideas are, indeed, out of place...." [16] The H. W. Johns Company agreed. "New dark body and trimming colors" were added to their cards "in consequence of the constantly increasing demand for the new styles of decoration." Johns claimed that they were the first company "to introduce the rich olive drabs, olive greens, maroons, etc., which are now so effectively and tastefully used in the decoration of ornamental villas, seaside hotels and other structures...." [17]

As the nineteenth century waned, American domestic architecture began to return to simpler lines inspired in part by our colonial past. With this revival, paint colors also changed. Body colors moved toward pastels; white again became the most popular trim color and even was used for sash. As early as 1893, the H. W. Johns Company, while still offering dark colors and stains for use on late Queen Anne and Shingle style houses, wrote that "the yellows which are so extensively used on Colonial and other styles of houses, should be trimmed with our Outside White." For shutters and sash, the company recommended dark green *or* white! "Body colors of light greys and other neutral tints may also be trimmed with White or Ivory White, using [the] same color for blinds and sash." [18]

By 1914, firms like the Lowe Brothers Paint Company (SEE, PLATES 79–90) were recommending that "trimming should be lighter than the house itself . . . , white or very light colors should be used for the trim," and "dark colors rarely look well." [19] In this period, nonetheless, the cornice, corner boards, and belt courses were still defined against the body color—even when the body was light yellow and the trim an ivory white. It would only be with the introduction of bungalows and later tract housing that Americans would be weaned away from multi-color paint schemes, the importance of enhancing niceties of architectural detail being lost in a flood of white paint.

COLOR PLACEMENT

Nearly all houses built in America prior to World War One were intended to be defined by the trimming color. Even a quick examination of the plates in this book will show the outlining of corner boards, cornice, water table and belt courses. All of these elements are usually painted in the major trim color. Then the main vertical and horizontal elements of the porches are outlined in the same fashion. Finally, the window and door openings are outlined. I favor a light body and dark trim, but this need not be a hard and fast rule; there is ample precedent for the opposite placement. However, keep in mind that a large house can be made to appear smaller by selecting a trim color that is darker than the main body color.

After the house has been fully outlined, additional colors may be introduced. The simpler the house, the fewer the colors is a good guideline to follow. Also, reversing the body color within major areas painted in the trim color is generally to be preferred over intro-

ducing a third major color (except on Queen Anne and other late Victorian houses). Cornice brackets and porch balusters, for example, usually look better painted in the body color against the trim. One area which causes many people problems is the brackets on Italianate roof and porch cornices. Usually these are painted out with the cornice. The exception to this rule is when the brackets are fabricated from three or more boards so there is a recessed face or recessed scroll on the sides. In those cases the recesses are usually picked out in the body color for contrast. The sash and shutters, however, will probably carry different colors. As a general rule, these two elements will be the darkest parts of the house. Especially on houses erected between 1840 and 1900, the sash will be darker than the trim, usually deep reddish or chocolate brown, dark green, olive, or even black. This gives the effect of the windows receding into the facade rather than projecting, which is exactly the effect that was intended. Many fine old-house paint schemes are spoiled at the last movement by painting the moveable sash white, the light body color, or, even more unhappily, by the application of white storm windows where the commercially available dark brown ones could have been used. Shutters, too, are usually darker. Often they are painted in the trim color with recessed panels picked out in the body color, or in an even darker shade of the body-trim combination. If the shutters are to be painted in the trim color, be sure to paint the backs of them in the body color (with the recessed panels picked out in the trim color) so when they are closed there will be definition between the window frames and the shutter rails. Little tricks such as this enliven a facade and show an understanding of how the nineteenth century used paint (SEE, PLATE 26).

On rare occasions the chamfering of porch posts and the *putty* of sash are painted in bright red, but it cannot be emphasized enough that excessive picking out is to be avoided. If you are uncertain, leave it off (SEE, PLATE 39). Especially in the late nineteenth and early twentieth centuries, classical decorations (wreaths garlands, swags) were often applied in the peaks of gables or around the drums of towers (SEE, PLATES 60 AND 75). These details were rarely picked out against the background and never like polychrome Della Robbia. American color schemes throughout the nineteenth century were relatively simple. Only in the late Victorian period, and especially on Queen Anne houses, did multi-color schemes for the body of the house become popular. The safest combination for houses of that period is a stack of dark to light shades of the same color applied with the darkest shade on the first floor, medium on the second floor, and the lightest on the third floor. Sherwin-Williams stated in their 1885 book, *What Color?*, "where it is desired to bring out or fully preserve the structural design, the projecting parts, called high lights, should be lighter in color than the receding or sunken parts, called shadows. Again, we should bear in mind that the parts nearest the ground should, by the use of darker colors, be made to look heavier than the higher parts, which, by use of lighter colors, prevent the structure from appearing top-heavy."[20]

COLOR CHOICE

Just as the Victorians had difficulty with the rich colors introduced for use on "the broken surfaces and picturesque outlines of the modern Queen Anne country house," so do owners of these same houses today. White trimmed with green is safe and clean looking. It requires no imagination, no originality, no spark of adventure, and certainly no sensitivity to the original intent of the builders who planned that the recessed and projecting elements or the varied textures of their designs would be complemented by carefully selected colors. In an essay on "Modern House Painting" published in 1884 by the H. W. Johns Paint Company, the author argued that: "The laudable and rapidly growing tendency to the free use of color in the decoration of villas and cottages as well as the most pretentious structures, warrants us in assuming that the 'white house with green blinds,' except as an occasional desirable variation, is a thing of the past, and we believe the new rich colors we manufacture will be appreciated by those who are desirous of beautifying their homes, at the same time securing in their appearance a greater degree of individuality than has hitherto obtained, and increasing the attractiveness of their villages, towns and suburbs, tenfold." [21]

Individuality. In addition to a historically sensitive color scheme, many owners of Victorian houses are seeking a form of self-expression. This has not been without its excesses. Recently a colorist movement, spawned largely by the owners of Victorian houses in San Francisco, has begun to spread across the country. This bright, gay, exuberant use of pastels calls attention to the visually exciting asymmetrical lines and varied textures of late nineteenth-century frame buildings. In too many cases, unfortunately, neither the choice of colors nor their placement on San Francisco's "painted ladies" is historically correct. In addition to the protection it offers, paint is a cosmetic. As any beautician will explain, the application of cosmetics is a subtle skill; the trick is to enhance the best features without calling attention to the effort.

It is easy enough to be critical of owners for repainting time after time in safe, clean white, or for

selecting freely from the wide range of boutique colors. But how is the average owner of a Victorian building to know what colors are correct and how they should be applied? Fortunately, as is shown in the following plates and on the color card supplied with this book, there is a wide range of colors that are historically acceptable. It is possible to express individuality and be fair to the history of the building. Such freedom, of course, is not available to persons responsible for interpreting museum houses. There every effort must be made to determine the original colors and to apply them as they were, even if the colors and their placement are inconsistent with the curator's or board's perception of good taste. If the building is not a museum, the owner has the entire world of the colorful Victorians open to him.

Victorian architectural critics and paint companies provided homeowners with painting guides and color chips, many of which are available in the research collections of institutions such as The Athenaeum of Philadelphia. Some house painting guides included line drawings to show how buildings should be painted; many of these guides contained colored plates, one hundred of which are reproduced in the pages that follow. A close examination of these plates shows the placement of the body, trim, and "picking out" colors. Color selection itself is more difficult because of the limited accuracy of nineteenth-century color printing. By the time modern copies are made of these plates, they become too unreliable for close color matches. These illustrations must be used together with color chips made from the actual paint. For that reason, forty reference color samples of the new Sherwin-Williams "Heritage Colors" line are supplied with this book. By comparing the plates and the samples it is possible to determine both placement and color. In addition, an "affinity" chart drawn from the same original sources is provided; it allows selection of those trim colors that the Victorians thought went best with each body color. This chart makes it possible for you to select a body color that you like, to which trim colors may be matched with reasonable assurance that the combination will be historically correct for your building, while, at the same time, reflecting your own color preferences. For example, if "Rookwood Jade" is selected as the body color of an 1880s house, the affinity chart shows that this color was usually trimmed with "Rookwood Blue Green," or, if a lighter trim is wanted, "Downing Sand" might be used. If "Renwick Yellow" is selected as the body color, the chart shows "Rookwood Antique Yellow" as a trim, but also four compatible grays, several browns, and even an olive.

Each of the historic color periods covered by this book represents a reaction to the color choices that went before and reflect pendulum-like swings of half a century: gradually darkening, then a return to lighter colors, followed by the current trend back to darker colors that first began to appear with the introduction of Williamsburg colonial colors in the post-World War Two years. This most recent darkening of paint colors has gradually found acceptance and happily coincides with the historic preservation movement. This has caused many people to look at buildings erected between 1820 and 1920 with a fresh eye, including the question of color. Since most of these structures date from the last period of richer color use, a considerable number of owners have adopted colorful paint schemes or are considering them. A case in point is the sea-side community of Cape May, New Jersey. The bulk of this handsome Landmark village's housing stock dates from the last quarter of the nineteenth century. These buildings have been uniformly painted in glaring white since the turn of the century. Interviews with elderly residents inevitably elicit the response that the Victorian, clapboard cottages, hotels, and churches have *"always"* been painted white." That is indeed true, *for their lifetimes*; by World War One the original dark colors of the 1870s and 1880s had been painted over. Close examination by microanalysis or even casual scraping reveals, however, that the first coats of paint on virtually all of these buildings were the browns, grays, reds, olives, yellows, and greens that became nearly universal in late Victorian America. Within the past year, several residents of Cape May, especially the inn keepers, have led a return to the colors intended by the original builders. One of these inns has been selected for the cover of this book. The few repainted buildings have so influenced the look of the historic district that a private home owner who recently repainted in colors admitted, "you can't paint in plain white anymore." He had learned from watching his more adventuresome neighbors that Americans have once again discovered the importance of paint for the exterior decoration of their homes; no longer will they accept the chromatic monotony of the past half century.

NOTES

1 Charles Dickens, *American Notes for General Circulation* (London, 1874), p. 81.

2 Andrew Jackson Downing, *Cottage Residences* (New York, 1842), pp. 22–23.

3 Andrew Jackson Downing, *The Architecture of Country Houses* (New York, 1850), pp. 198–206.

4 *Ibid.*

5 *Ibid.*, p. 204.

6 Henry William Cleaveland, William Backus and Samuel Backus, *Village and Farm Cottages* (New York, 1856); Gervase Wheeler, *Rural Homes* (New York, 1851); M. Field, *Rural Architecture* (New York, 1857); and Calvert Vaux, *Villas and Cottages* (New York, 1857).

7 "Art in House Painting," *Exterior Decoration* (New York, 1885), p. 18 of the reprinted edition (Philadelphia, 1976).

8 John Riddell, *Architectural Designs for Model Country Residences* (Philadelphia, 1861). Later editions appeared in 1864 and 1867.

9 For a bibliography of trade catalogues, see: Lawrence B. Romaine, *A Guide to American Trade Catalogs, 1744–1900* (New York, 1960).

10 C. P. Sherwood, *A Few Words About Paint and Painting* (Wadsworth, Martinez & Longman Co., c. 1884).

11 Isaac H. Hobbs, *Hobb's Architecture* (Philadelphia, Second Edition, 1876), p. 150.

12 Henry Hudson Holly, *Modern Dwellings in Town and Country* (New York, 1878), p. 27.

13 *Ibid.*, p. 26.

14 *Every Man His Own Painter!* or, *Paints—How to Select and Use Them* (Philadelphia, 1873), p. 6.

15 *Exterior Decoration*, p. 19.

16 E. K. Rossiter and F. A. Wright, *Modern House Painting* (New York, 1882), pp. 6–7.

17 H. W. Johns Company, *Structural Decoration* (1884), p. 6.

18 H. W. Johns Company, *Suggestions for Exterior Decoration* (1893), pp. 2–3.

19 Lowe Brothers Company, *The House Outside & Inside: How to Make Your Home Attractive* (Dayton, O., 1914).

20 Sherwin-Williams Company, *What Color?* (Cleveland, 1885), pp. 18–19.

21 H. W. Johns Company, *Structural Decoration* (1884), p. 1.

THE PLATES

The one hundred color plates that follow have all been reproduced from original documents in the collections of The Athenaeum of Philadelphia. The source for each plate is given in the caption in short form. The full bibliographical references are as follows:

Devoe, F. W. & Company, *Exterior Decoration* (New York, 1885), reprinted as *Exterior Decoration: Victorian Colors for Victorian Houses* (Philadelphia, The Athenaeum, 1976).

Downing, Andrew J., *Cottage Residences* (New York, 1842)

Heath & Milligan Manufacturing Co., *Best Prepared Paints* (Chicago, c. 1885).

Heath & Milligan Manufacturing Co., *Best Prepared Paints Ready for Use* (Chicago, c. 1890).

Johns, H. W. Manufacturing Co., *Artistic House Painting* (New York, 1895).

Johns, H. W. Manufacturing Co., *Structural Decoration* (New York, 1884).

Lowe Brothers Co., *The House Outside & Inside: How to Make Your Home Attractive* (Dayton, Ohio, 1914).

Lucas, John & Co., *Portfolio of Modern House Painting Designs* (Philadelphia, 1887).

Lugar, Robert. *Villa Architecture* (London, 1828).

Masury, John W. & Co., [Loose portfolio of mounted color plates] (New York & Chicago, c. 1910).

Papworth, J. B. *Designs for Rural Residences* (London, 1818).

Patton Paint Co., *Paints for All Purposes* (Milwaukee, Wis. & Newark, N. J., c. 1915).

Riddell, John. *Architectural Designs for Model Country Residences* (Philadelphia, 1861).

Rossiter, E. K. and F. A. Wright. *Modern House Painting* (New York, 1882).

Seeley Brothers. *Averill Paint* (New York, c. 1880).

Sherwin-Williams Co. *Catalogue of Paint and Colors for Railway Use* (Cleveland, 1885).

Sherwin-Williams Co. *Color Applied to Architecture* (Cleveland, 1887, 1888).

Sherwin-Williams Co. *House Painting: the Best Materials and Methods, Harmony of Colors and Correct Combinations* (Cleveland, 1884).

PLATE 1   In 1885 the Devoe Paint Company wrote of this plate, "the old style country dwelling, typical in its lack of all architectural ornamentation of the plain tastes and habits of the early settlers in the New England States, and of which many are still to be found, is here depicted treated in conventional style—painted white with green blinds. The cold, glaring effect is always harsh amid any surroundings, but the form of the house has been regarded as almost prohibitory of any attempt at artistic treatment." That a major paint company still found it necessary to complain about white trimmed with green several decades after architectural critics began to call for the use of color is indicative of the persistence of this scheme into the post-Centennial years.

(Devoe, *Exterior Decoration*, 1885)

PLATE 2   Designed as a summer cottage for P. B. Ainslie of Liverpool, this late Regency house shows many of the picturesque features which became common in American rural architecture in the hands of Downing and Notman in the 1840s. The soft coloring shown here is typical of the period as harsh white gave way to softer coloring.   (Lugar, *Villa Architecture*, 1828)

PLATE 3   Early nineteenth-century English architects introduced the soft coloring adopted by Downing and other American critics. This "Cottage Orne" was designed by John B. Papworth "to harmonize with garden scenery, and to afford a degree of embellishment by its verandahs and the variety of shadow which they project."   (Papworth, *Rural Residences*, 1828)

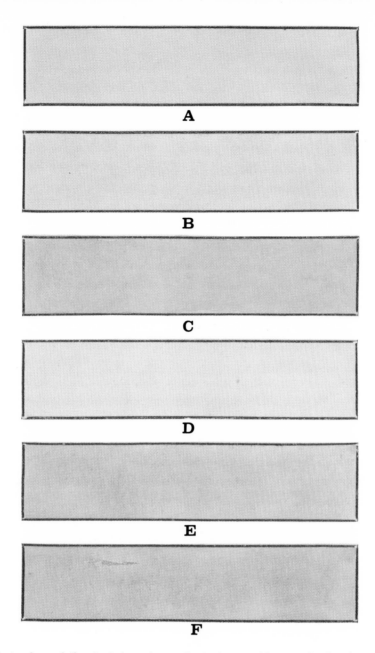

A

B

C

D

E

F

PLATE 4   One of the first American efforts to provide actual color in a book on architecture was Andrew Jackson Downing's hand-colored plate in *Cottage Residences* (New York, 1842). "As it is difficult to convey in words a proper idea of delicate shades of colour," he wrote, "and as we think the subject one of very great importance in domestic architecture, we have given specimens...of six shades of colour highly suitable for the exterior of cottages and villas. A, B, and C, are shades of gray, and E, F, G, of drab or fawn colour; which will be found pleasing and harmonious in any situation in the country. Stuccoed or cemented buildings should be marked off in courses, and tinted to resemble some mellow stone; Bath, Portland stone, or any other of the light free-stone shades, are generally most agreeable."

19

PLATE 5   The pale colors advocated by Downing and other architectural critics of the mid-nineteenth century are best shown in a rare series of plates published in 1861 by the Philadelphia architect John Riddell in a book entitled *Architectural Designs for Model Country Residences, Illustrated by Colored Drawings.* . . . Riddell selected "suitable tints" for the houses he illustrated which should be taken as general guidelines for these restrained Italianate villas of the 1850s. Later illustrations (plates 15 and 16) show the same style executed in the darker colors of the 1870s and 1880s.   (Riddell, *Architectural Designs*, 1861)

PLATE 6   This Italianate villa which cost $9,000 was designed for a Philadelphia doctor by John Riddell. Unlike the house illustrated in plate 5, the architect here suggests the introduction of a third color (in addition to the body and trim colors) for the sash. Generally the trend was toward ever darker sash until 1900. The Athenaeum of Philadelphia, for example, had already gone to dark brown sash by 1847. Riddell appears to recommend that the porch be picked out with the body color. Notice also the grained front doors.

(Riddell, *Architectural Designs*, 1861)

PLATE 7 There are several instructive details in this illustration of "a very neat and convenient house for a moderate sized family, wishing to live in the suburbs of a large city or town." The second story blinds are differently colored from those on the ground floor; the front door is grained in oak; and the tin porch roof is striped, a common practice when the roof was to be visible. The draperies are different colors to illustrate how each would look from the outside; the architect was not suggesting some form of bizarre decorative treatment.

(Riddell, *Architectural Designs*, 1861)

PLATE 8 For this house erected in Germantown near Philadelphia, we have the painting specifications: "All the good work, exterior and interior, that is to be painted, is to have three good coats of pure lead and linseed oil, the linseed oil is to be of good quality. The handrails, newels, and balusters are to have two good coats of good clean varnish; all the glass throughout the building is to be of good quality of thick American glass; and to be well fastened and puttied in the sash. All the tin of the roofs is to receive three good coats of good paint, one on the underside before put on, and two on the upper side; *the roof of the veranda is to be striped; all the lower story doors, and front sash, are to be grained in oak, pivot blinds and wire screens to be green,* kitchen wood work to be straw color." [Emphasis added] (Riddell, *Architectural Designs*, 1861)

PLATE 8

PLATE 9 This "neat and convenient homestead" costing $5,150 shows several details observed on earlier illustrations: bright green blinds on the second floor, oak grained front door, striped porch roof, light-colored sash and side-light frames (which may have been intended to be grained). Notice how the green of the blinds is used for the scalloped trim which covers the porch flashing and the color contrast of the stucco quoins on the corners. The banding of the lantern trim is an interesting detail which enlivens the entire composition.

(Riddell, *Architectural Designs*, 1861)

PLATE 10   This small Gothic cottage relies heavily for effect on its ornamental barge board, cut from two-inch-thick white pine, the striped roof and its scalloped flashing. The white trim stands out against the pale stucco of the body, but the pink, blue, and green of the roof holds the key to the success of this composition. Notice how important the choices of pink and blue draperies are to the overall effect.   (Riddell, *Architectural Designs*, 1861)

PLATE 11   This cottage owes much to the Regency designs of early nineteenth-century England. The veranda pilasters, ornaments, the window heads and sills, were all to be executed in cast iron. As in previous figures, the striped roof, light sash, green blinds, and grained doors are critical to the entire composition; without these the house would appear plain and uninteresting.

(Riddell, *Architectural Designs*, 1861)

PLATE 12   Issued in the late 1860s, the F. W. Devoe paint card of "Homestead Colors" is one of the earliest examples in America of this soon to be ubiquitous advertising form. The colors shown are somewhat darker than those illustrated by Downing or Riddell. Notice the sanded examples. For reference purposes, the chips have been matched to the Munsell System color notation by Frank S. Welsh, historic paint color specialist, Bryn Mawr, PA.

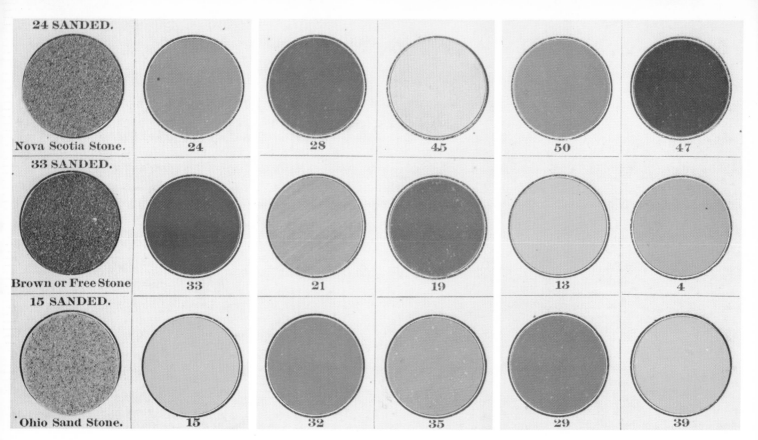

PLATE 12

The original chips were coated with a clear oil-resin varnish for protection which has yellowed with age. This varnish was removed in a small area to expose the original color for matching to the Munsell System.

Color Number	Munsell Notation	Neighboring Munsell Standards
24	10 Y 6.5/1*	10 Y 7/1 & 10 Y 6/1
33	4 YR 4.5/2*	5 YR 5/2 & 2.5 YR 4/2
15	5 Y 8/1	
28	5 YR 5.2/1*	5 YR 5/1 & 5 YR 6/1
21	10 YR 7/1.8*	10 YR 7/1 & 10 YR 7/2
32	6 YR 6/1.75*	5 YR 6/1 & 7.5 YR 6/2
45	1 Y 8.2/1.5*	10 YR 8/1 & 2.5 Y 8.5/2
19	7 YR 4.5/3.5*	7.5 YR 5/4 & 5 YR 5/2
35	9 YR 7/3.5*	10 YR 7/4 & 10 YR 7/2
50	8.5 YR 6/1.5*	10 YR 6/1 & 10 YR 6/2
13	10 Y 7.2/1.8*	10 Y 7/1 & 10 Y 8/2
29	10 YR 5.5/2*	10 YR 5/2 & 10 YR 6/2
47	2 Y 4/2*	10 YR 4/2 & 2.5 Y 4/2
4	5 B 7/0.5*	5 B 7/1 & N 7.0/
39	N 8.0/	

*indicates an estimated notation

Estimated Munsell Notations: When a paint color does not exactly match one of the regularly produced Munsell color standards in their color books, then the paints' color notation must be estimated between the two closest neighboring standards.

PLATE 13

Color Number	National Bureau of Standards Color Names	Munsell Notation	Color Number	National Bureau of Standards Color Names	Munsell Notation
1	Dark Green	7.5 G 3/4	29	Moderate Yellowish Pink	7.5 R 7/4
3	Grayish Blue	5 PB 4/2	31	Dark Grayish Reddish Brown	7.5 R 2/2
4	Grayish Blue	2.5 PB 5/4	34	Grayish Red	7.5 R 5/2
5	Bluish Gray	10 B 6/1	35	Strong Reddish Brown	10 R 3/10
6	Light Yellowish Green	2.5 G 7/4	36	Deep Reddish Orange	7.5 R 4/12
7	Strong Yellowish Brown	7.5 YR 5/6	37	Moderate Reddish Orange	1.5 YR 5/10
8	Dark Orange Yellow	8.5 YR 5.5/8	38	Dark Orange Yellow	7.5 YR 6.3/10
10	Dark Orange Yellow	7.5 YR 6/8	39	Brilliant Yellow	5 Y 8/10
11	Moderate Orange Yellow	7.5 YR 7/6	40	Pale Greenish Yellow	10 Y 8.5/4
12	Pale Orange Yellow	9 YR 7.5/4	41	Yellowish White	5 Y 9/0.5
13	Grayish Reddish Brown	10 R 3/2	42	Deep Yellowish Green	10 GY 4/8
15	Grayish Brown	7.5 YR 3/2	43	Yellowish Gray	10 Y 7.5/1
16	Grayish Brown	7.5 YR 4/2	44	Yellowish White	2.5 Y 8.5/2
17	Light Grayish Brown	7.5 YR 5/3	45	Yellowish Gray	8 YR 7/2
19	Moderate Olive Brown	2.5 Y 3/2	46	Yellowish Gray	2.5 Y 8/2
20	Grayish Olive	5 Y 4/2	47	Grayish Yellow	3.5 Y 8/3
21	Olive Gray	5 Y 4/1	48	Pale Yellowish Pink	7.5 YR 8/2
22	Light Olive Brown	2.5 Y 4.5/2	49	Light Neutral Gray	N 8.0/
23	Light Grayish Yellowish Brown	10 YR 6/2	50	Light Bluish Green	5 BG 7.3/4
25	Moderate Reddish Brown	7.5 R 3/6	51	Grayish Reddish Brown	7.5 R 3.5/2
28	Grayish Red	5 R 5/4	52	Pinkish Gray	10 R 7/1

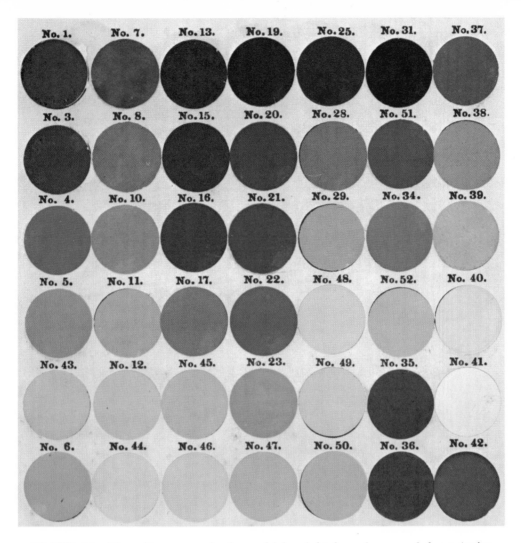

PLATE 14 The wide range of colors which might have been used for exterior decoration in the late 1860s and early 1870s is well illustrated in this rare Harrison Brothers "Town and Country" paint card of 1871. The pale Downing colors survive together with the darker palette that will dominate the next twenty years. For reference purposes, the chips have been matched to the Munsell System color notation and given National Bureau of Standards color names by Frank S. Welsh, historic paint specialist, Bryn Mawr, PA.

 The original chips were coated with a clear oil-resin varnish for protection which has yellowed with age. This varnish was removed in a small area to expose the original color for matching to the Munsell System.

PLATE 15 As colors darkened in the last quarter of the nineteenth century, paint companies showed how older houses, such as this "style of building first erected in the Eastern and Middle States about twenty-five years ago," could be repainted "to produce a somewhat more substantial effect" than was possible with "the original white and delicate neutral tints."

(Devoe, *Exterior Decoration*, 1885)

PLATE 16   The same Italianate house illustrated in plate 15 is shown here with
a "combination of colors . . . intended to give it a richer, warmer appearance. Four
colors are used here (and on plate 15) : body, trim, blinds, and sash.

(Devoe, *Exterior Decoration*, 1885)

PLATE 17

PLATE 18   The suggested color scheme for this "plain, comfortable village residence" illustrates that late nineteenth-century houses need not always be painted
in dark colors. Comparison with the "Heritage Colors" sample card supplied with
this book will show that the body color, Rookwood Antique Gold ("one of the
tints which the ladies call 'perfectly lovely'"), and the trim color, Renwick Gold
("a beautiful light buff, much used"), are somewhat darker than the printed
plate suggests. Only the front door, porch, and step treads are shown painted a
dark reddish brown. Normally the dark brown would also appear on the sash and
the body color would be used on the brackets and decorative work in the gables.
(Sherwin-Williams, *Color Applied to Architecture*, 1888)

PLATE 17   On this plate, showing a mid-nineteenth-century Italianate house, a
dark yellow body has been trimmed with a lighter yellow. There is no picking out
on the porch, but the sunk face on the sides of the cornice bracket and the recessed
panel in the cornice frieze have been painted in the body color. Normally the sunk
face of the cornice bracket *edge* would also be picked out. Similar treatment would
be appropriate and is often found on the porch brackets. As would be expected, the
sash and front doors are a dark color, here a brownish orange.
(Sherwin-Williams, *Color Applied to Architecture*, 1887)

PLATE 19   In contrast to the simpler house illustrated in plate 18, this house has been painted in two yellows and a moderate yellowish brown to bring out the various textures, especially in the attic gables. A dark brown might also be used on the sash to good effect. As a general rule, *the sash of Victorian houses should be the darkest detail so that the windows appear to recede into the facade.* If lighter colors than the window frames are used for the sash, the windows are given more prominence. A close examination of the plates in this book amply illustrate this principle. Fortunately, dark brown storm windows are now available; they are more appropriate than the more common white.

(Sherwin-Williams, *Color Applied to Architecture*, 1888)

PLATE 20   As a general rule, the less complex the trimmings of a house are, the fewer colors should be used. Here body and trim colors have been reversed to enliven an otherwise plain farm house where the introduction of an additional color would not have been appropriate. On the porches the recessed panels of the doors, the brackets, the soffits, the abacus and base moldings of the posts, and the flat balusters have been picked out in the body color against the trim color. The trim color has also been used on the crown molding of the brick chimney caps and to outline the panel molding below the porches. The ceilings under the eaves are shown in shadow, but properly should be painted in the body color. The design for this house first appeared in a book by the New York architect E. C. Hussey titled *Home Building* (1876). "Its prototype," wrote Hussey, "may be seen pleasantly reposing amid the shadows of well-grown trees, or rigidly enduring the blaze of a new, unplanted lot, on the streets and avenues of hundreds of recently built towns and cities from the Atlantic to the Pacific."   (*Seeley Brothers*, 1886)

PLATE 20

PLATE 21 This plate shows "an inexpensive country or village house, estimated cost $800," which was, "five or ten years ago invariably painted white, with green blinds." In this perspective view the body of the house has been painted a dark color and the trim lighter. Note that two additional colors have carefully been introduced for the recessed panels of the shutters and all sash, otherwise the modest trim is not picked out. The porch brackets, rafter projections under the eaves, and the porch post moldings are painted the main trim color.   (*Lucas,* 1887)

PLATE 22 The front elevation of the house from plate 21 shows the effect of reversing the *same* colors, now used as a light body and dark trim. The shutters are painted to match the trim with the sash color used to pick out door and first floor shutter moldings. Notice that the porch brackets are painted with the trim, not picked out.   (*Lucas*, 1887)

PLATE 23   Here is "a prevalent style of American country dwelling of reasonable cost, about $1000. The general effect of this design is quite in accord with
accepted schemes for painting such properties in most sections of the country." As
might be expected, the cornice, including the brackets which are probably without
recessed faces or carving, is entirely painted in the trim color. The trim color has
also been introduced in the grills under the porch, while the body color has been
used on the shutter and door panels to provide some variety.   (*Lucas*, 1887)

PLATE 24   The side view of the house from plate 23 reverses the same colors. The effect is rather more dramatic since the barge boards and brackets now stand out against the lighter body, but this may reflect the author's particular prejudice for trim that is darker than the body color.   (*Lucas*, 1887)

PLATE 25   This is the same house shown in Plate 1 updated to the 1880s! "At an expense of about twenty-five or thirty dollars belt courses of four-inch tongue and groove boarding have been substituted for sections of the clap-boarding of our old-fashioned house, effectively breaking up the flat side-wall surfaces, allowing of a contrast in color and effect between the first and second stories, and architecturally changing the entire appearance of the structure." First story, Rookwood Red; second story, Rookwood Dark Olive; belt course, Rookwood Terra Cotta (Trim); shutters, Rookwood Shutter Green; sash, Rookwood Dark Red (Trim).   (Devoe Paint Company, *Exterior Decoration*, 1885)

PLATE 26   The Lucas Paint Company called this a "primative form of cottage, which the traveler notices in various portions of the United States. . . . The colors used . . . are not only well adapted to country residences, but are especially recommended for the small, portable or colonization buildings, that are manufactured for exportation in the New England States and elsewhere." Estimated cost of this house was given as $3,000. In particular, note that the *open* sides of the shutters are painted with the body color on the panels and slats, while on the *closed* side the same elements are painted to match the trim. This reversal allows for color separation even when some shutters are open and others closed. This subtle detail should be followed in all paint schemes where there is a color difference between the slats and frame.   (*Lucas*, 1887)

PLATE 27 "The usual style of American Country or Village House, roomy and convenient; easily erected, and quite popular. Cost estimated, $2,800." Notice that the ceilings under the eaves are painted in the body color, while the entire cornice, *except the dentils*, is painted in the trim color. Both the grills under the porch and the panels of the front door are picked out in the body color against the darker trim.

(*Lucas*, 1887)

PLATE 28 Here the body and trim colors shown in plate 27 have been reversed on what is essentially the same building. The dentils of the cornice and the grills under the porch are painted in the trim color to match. (*Lucas*, 1887)

PLATE 29

PLATE 30

PLATE 31 "The residence here shown, of excellent proportions and erected in an attractive style of architecture, is located in Connecticut and situated at such an elevation and with such open surroundings as to have from almost all points of view, the sky as a background. Painted in light neutral shades it presented a cold, unsubstantial appearance, and in order to give it an air of warmth and solidity, and at the same time a certain cheerful prominence, the colors shown in our design were suggested."   (Devoe Paint Company, *Exterior Decoration*, 1885)

PLATE 29 This late Gothic, story and a half cottage is here shown in the darker colors of the 1880s. Notice the subtle picking out with red on the sash, panel moldings above and below the bay windows, and the panel moldings on the front doors. The temptation to use red on the porch cornice, brackets, or on the barge boards should be resisted. One detail not seen on earlier plates, however, is the way the window bay projection has been made more prominent by painting all of main elements in the trim color, then picking out the trim and sash in the body color.
(*Lucas*, 1887)

PLATE 30 In this side elevation of the house shown in plate 29, the body color has been used on the decorative trim of the porch. Again the body and trim colors have been reversed on the bay (shown in profile to the left side of the plate) instead of being painted out with the clapboards of the body and trimmed as the rest of the windows.
(*Lucas*, 1887)

PLATES 32 AND 33   These two plates show alternative schemes for simple houses
being repainted in the 1880s. Of particular value is the detailed picking out of
horizontal and vertical members which should be studied closely before beginning
to paint in any colors. "Two designs are shown; one, the typical French roof house,
and the other a story and one-half gabled cottage, also typical of a very large class.

Only a portion of each house is shown; just enough to properly indicate the painting. There are no shingles that can receive stains, and sombre colorings that are in place on other designs would here produce a heavy and unwieldy effect. Especially is this true of the French roof design. The cottage can receive freer treatment."

(Rossiter & Wright, *Modern House Painting*, 1883)

PLATE 34 A "familiar style American suburban residence with Mansard roof. A pleasant departure from the old rectangular design with peaked roof. Estimated cost, $2,800." This scheme emphasizes the importance of painting all vertical and horizontal trim elements which suggest structure. Here the strength of the upward thrust from foundation to the cornice brackets, which appear to support the roof, is intensified by the dark trim against the lighter body. Note the use of trim color in dormer cheeks and pediments. The trim color also enhances the brackets and recessed panels of the cornice against a soffit and frieze painted in the body color. The porch grill screens are here painted out with the trim color, and the front door panels are executed in the body color. (*Lucas*, 1887)

PLATE 35 In 1875, the architect Elisha Charles Hussey boarded a transcontinental train to survey the state of American architecture. The resulting book, *Home Building ... from New York to San Francisco* (New York, 1876), contained 42 plates. A decade later, Seeley Brothers Paint Company recycled several of Hussey's designs as full-color lithographs. These plates, six of which are reproduced on the following pages, are among the most informative to survive for details of late Victorian exterior decoration. The quotations in the captions are from Hussey's book.

Plate 35 illustrates a Mansardic villa (called a "turreted French-roof villa") painted in five colors. There is more picking out of details here than on any other house illustrated in this book. Typically for the period, the sash color is a rich, dark red; but in addition, the sash color has been used to highlight the trim: on the finials and the faces of the console brackets projecting from the cheeks of the dormers, on the dentils and patera of the roof, on the raised moldings and bracket faces of the balcony, and so on down to the panels under the porch. In spite of the use of red for a picking out color, the most important effects are achieved by reversing the body and main trim colors.

(Seeley Brothers, 1886)

PLATE 36 In contrast to the villa shown in plate 35, which is picked out in bright red, the third color introduced onto this Mansardic house is a much deeper shade. "The piazzas incline to plainness, the main cornice is moderately ornamented, and the deck is set with small brackets, and carries over it an iron cresting and finials, which greatly embellishes it, and breaks up all harshness of the sky lines." Body and trim colors are reversed in the conventional manner, but the touch of dark red shows on the dormer console brackets, cornice bracket faces, the scalloped frieze in the cornice, the patera below each bracket, and the sash. Notice also the use of body and trim colors on the chimney shaft and cap. The scale of this plate is too small to show that picking out on cornice bracket faces is normally confined to those which are built up in layers to create a sunken face in the center (*see* architectural terms, numbers 15 and 16). When this occurs, the sunken face and the raised faces are usually painted different colors. *(Seeley Brothers, 1886)*

PLATE 37 Darker colors, especially when the vertical and horizontal trimmings are carefully picked out, generally make a house appear smaller, as on this villa in "a sort of an Americanized Gothic style." A third color is also used here for bargeboards, scalloped friezes, and porch brackets, with just a touch of red picking out the patera on the bargeboards and porch brackets. "The frilled drapery," Hussey writes, "passes entirely around the gables and eaves, effectually breaking up the harshness so common to straight cornice lines. . . . The eaves project 3 feet 6 inches, which is very heavy, and, in consequence, are cut out on scrolled

lines, over the side windows, to let in sunlight, and remove all unpleasant stiffness of appearance." In Hussey's original design, he calls for "an iron cresting, of the 'Yates' pattern, painted a deep sky-blue, with all the tips gilded." Notice how important the two-color slate roof is to the entire composition. Study closely the reversal of body and trim colors on the window bays that add "very much to the exterior richness of effect." *(Seeley Brothers, 1886)*

PLATE 38 "The building represented in this plate was designed for Summer use at one of our seaside watering resorts. It is, however, just as it is shown in this plate, admirably adapted for street use in most of the picturesque little cities and towns of California. Its exterior form and ornamentation is of the Swiss style, although the stories are higher than are generally used in Swiss buildings. The almost excessive frill work gives it a very pretty, although a rather tawdry appearance." To emphasize different textures, two body colors are shown: the darker, as is usual, on the first floor, lighter on the shingled second floor. A third and even lighter color is used for all of the trim, excepting the roof cresting. Notice that the exuberant trim is *not* picked out; its light color against the darker body provides adequate definition. The first floor body color and the trim color are reversed on the doors, step base moldings, panels, risers, posts, and behind the porch lattice work. *(Seeley Brothers, 1886)*

PLATE 39 Picking out in bright colors was relatively rare in the third quarter of the nineteenth century, notwithstanding the evidence of this plate. The Seeley Brothers Company seems consistently to have advocated gayer treatments than Sherwin-Williams, Devoe, or Lucas. On this villa, "erected at West Rutherford, N. J., within the past few months," the defining outline of horizontal and vertical trim (water table, belt course, corner boards, etc.) is strongly emphasized against the light body color. A third color has been introduced to pick out roof finials, the face of cornice brackets, sash, balcony balusters, patera (the flat, round disks), porch brackets, abacus, etc. Colors for this amount of picking out should not be too bright. Deeper reds than are suggested by the plate would be more appropriate than bright scarlet.

(Seeley Brothers, 1886)

PLATE 40 This "Swedo-Gothic model" villa is reproduced to to illustrate the treatment of the ceiling under the eaves where recessed panels are painted in the body color, defined by the trim. Notice also how the trim color carries up to the gable and dormer, strongly outlining the highly decorative features of both. On a house of this design, the ground floor is normally painted a darker color than the upper floor, separated by the belt course in the trim color.

(Seeley Brothers, 1886)

PLATE 35

PLATE 36

SEELEY BROS'

NEW YORK.

BOSTON.

CHICAGO.

PLATE 37

PLATE 38

SEELEY BROS' NEW YORK.
BOSTON.
CHICAGO

PLATE 39

PLATE 40

PLATE 41

PLATE 42

PLATE 43

PLATES 41 TO 44   In the 1880s, the Heath & Milligan Manufacturing Company of Chicago issued sample books of "fashionable tints" to show "the appearance of a house when painted with any of our shades." A range of examples from the earlier of these books is reproduced here. The house selected is a relatively simple, vernacular box that has been enriched by incised decoration on the window frames, belt course, and barge boards. The body colors illustrated range from yellow trimmed with green, through light gray trimmed with light brown, two shades of green, and dark green trimmed with olive. The gray-brown combination in particular shows how persistent the lighter colors advocated by Downing in the 1840s proved to be.

PLATE 44

PLATE 45

PLATES 45 TO 48 For a later sample book, Heath & Milligan selected the flank elevation of a large Queen Anne house. The plates are especially good illustrations for the complex pattern of horizontal and vertical trim elements, particularly on the tower. (*Heath & Milligan Manufacturing Company*, c. 1885)

PLATE 46

PLATE 47

PLATE 48

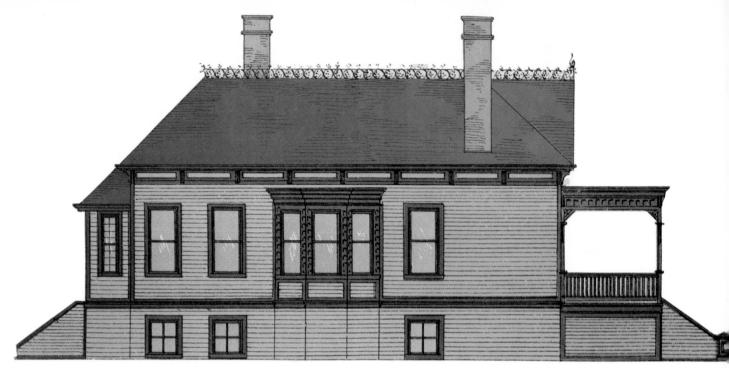

PLATE 50

PLATE 51   PLATE 52

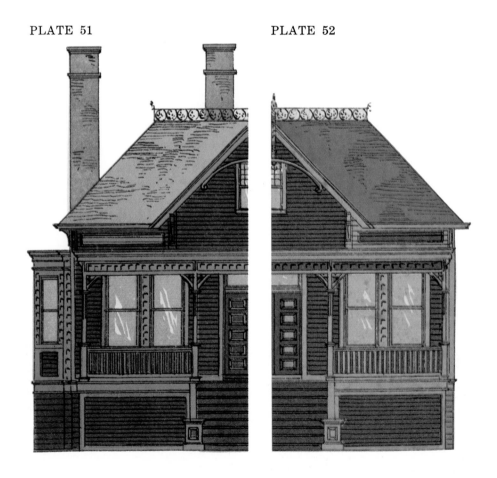

PLATE 49   The cottage shown here and in plates 50, 51, and 52 is "a general favorite on the Western coast of the United States, especially in California, where many of them may be seen with their artistic gables, bay windows and porches, entwined with roses and other creeping vines, relieved against the luxuriant verdure of the picturesque landscape." Estimated cost of building, $2,800. Appropriately for a simple house, only a body and single trim color are used. Of particular interest is the carrying of the body color right up to the crown molding. The cornice brackets are painted in the body color; however, the trim color is introduced into the recessed panels of the cornice on both the main body of the house and the porch.   (*Lucas*, 1887)

PLATE 50   In this side view of the house from plate 49, the light/dark relationship of body and trim colors has been reversed. Now the body color is carried into the recessed panels of the cornice, but no picking out is shown on the porch. This treatment provides a stronger outline for the house.   (*Lucas*, 1887)

PLATES 51 AND 52   Here are two schemes for the front elevation of the house shown in plate 49. The greater contrast in plate 52 emphasizes the simple decoration of the gable and porch. Although it is not illustrated on this plate, dark sash in the light window frames would be appropriate.   (*Lucas*, 1887)

PLATE 53

PLATE 54

PLATE 55   "This design is presented as a fair example of a modern Queen Anne wooden house. It may stand as a type for a house of a more expensive nature. . . . The decorative idea underlying the painting as shown in the plate, consists in grading the colors from heavy rich shades at the bottom, up through a middle harmony to the lighter tones of the gable peaks. The tones used for this purpose are warm and rich. The trimmings, on the contrary, are painted a cooler color, giving great strength of contrast, and emphasizing the body colors. . . . A building of this class ought not to have outside blinds. The arrangement of the windows is such that outside blinds cannot be open without shutting against other windows. The ordinary inside blind would be better, and best of all the Venetian blind. If outside blinds should be used they had best be painted a color that closely approaches the middle tint, and also the body color of the first story."

(Rossiter and Wright, *Modern House Painting*, 1883)

PLATES 53 AND 54   "A charming design for a low-cost cottage, which could be built for about $1,000—a grateful improvement on the old order of village building." A comparison of these two perspectives demonstrate how important *placement* is, regardless of the colors selected. On plate 54, most of the body is painted in the same color. In plate 53, however, the trim color is carried to the gables and the drum of the tower. The effect is strikingly different. The change of color on the conical roof and the eyebrow dormer contributes greatly to the success of the decoration; such an effect could easily be achieved when reroofing, even in modern materials, at no additional cost.   (*Lucas*, 1887)

63

PLATE 56 Concerning this plate, Rossiter and Wright remarked that "the trimmings of a house are usually painted in a darker color than the body, the idea
being, no doubt, that those parts of the house which denote in some measure its
construction, should be emphasized in painting. But, a great deal that a painter is
apt to deal with as 'trimmings' is anything but constructional in character, and
should not be emphasized from any point of view. Take a house, for instance,
devoid of anything but vicious ornamentation—gimcracks and stuck-on ornaments
bearing no relation to the construction. Here, if the painter is left to follow the
rule, the result will be an enhancement of the defects, for the very things that it
would be good taste to screen as far as possible by uniformity of one color, will
only stand out more prominently." This is not to suggest that the authors were
opposed to the use of multiple colors. "In this plate the trimmings are made a
lighter color, and the body colors are dark. The effect of a house painted after the
scheme shown here would be extremely rich and elegant."

(Rossiter and Wright, *Modern House Painting*, 1883)

PLATE 57   This "pretty little cottage" has been given a green first story (such as Rookwood Jade) and a yellow second story (such as Renwick Yellow). "This would be an effective and bright composition for a small tree embowered cottage; the contrasts of color are strong, but being in the dulled scale they are not too striking for this kind of a design. On a different kind of a building it might not answer at all. It must be borne in mind that all buildings cannot be treated alike. The colorings that with some designs would be very effective, on others would be out of keeping. The fact is that a house should be painted so that its salient features of form and detail will be enhanced. The coloring should be subordinated to the design."   (Rossiter and Wright, *Modern House Painting*, 1883)

PLATE 58 This plate "represents a section of a new and pleasing Queen Anne cottage, where a different color is used in painting each story of the house." Rookwood Dark Red (Trim) is used on the body of the first story; Rookwood Olive on the body of the second story; Renwick Yellow on the body of the attic; Rookwood Amber (Trim) is used for the principal trimmings; Rookwood Red for the carved panels and chimneys; Rookwood Olive for the steps. The sash on the first story is black, and the other two stories, Rookwood Dark Red (Trim). An alternative scheme might be Rookwood Medium Brown (Trim) for the body of the first story; Rookwood Olive, body of the second story; and Rookwood Blue Green for body of the attic; Rookwood Red, for the principal trimmings. "We strongly recommend," wrote The Sherwin-Williams Company, "the use of three body colors for painting this style of architecture; still there are a few that do not care to keep pace with the improvements in exterior painting, and cling to the old way of using only one color for the entire body of the house."
(Sherwin-Williams Paint Company, *House Painting*, 1884)

PLATE 59 This detail of a Queen Anne cottage shows a typical three color body scheme of the 1880s, unified by a principal trim color which picks out the vertical and horizontal elements. Note the use of black for the sash throughout. A combination which might be tried for this house would be: body, first story, Rookwood Medium Brown (Trim); trimming first story, frame work in gable, ridge roll, water table, belt course and window frame in second story, Tiffany Bronze; second story and gable panels, Rookwood Terra Cotta (Trim). Another combination might be: first story body, Rookwood Dark Olive; trimming, Rookwood Olive; gable panels, Rookwood Amber (Trim); second story body, Rookwood Red.
(Sherwin-Williams Paint Company, *Color Applied to Architecture*, 1888)

PLATE 59

67

PLATE 60   A hint of classical revival detailing was just beginning to appear on this "modern design" shown "in colors of more subdued nature" which produced a "tasty effect." The design was by the Philadelphia architect F. H. Dodge, about which the Lucas Paint Company wrote, "it is seldom that an architect succeeds in producing such a pleasing and commodious design for a modern cottage, at so low an estimate for building, the cost being about $6,000." Starting with a dark body, the stuccoed areas of the gables are given a strong contrasting color. A third color is introduced for all trim, including the half timbering, the scroll pedimented dormer, and the applied classical decoration on the balcony. Opinion was divided on whether such applied decorations should be highlighted, but by the early twentieth century most sources show them painted out with the background. The author has rarely seen such highlighting of trim attempted successfully; it is never successful *when executed in more than one color against the background.*

(*Lucas*, 1887)

PLATE 61   With its late Victorian tower, Shingle Style massing, and comfortable Colonial Revival veranda, this house might be painted in one of the lighter greens (Tiffany Palm Green), trimmed with olive (Rookwood Olive) which is shown here also used on the sash and shutters.

(H. W. Johns Manufacturing Company, *Artistic House Painting*, 1895)

PLATE 62

PLATE 63   Many shingled houses were erected in the United States at the end
of the nineteenth century. Normally it was recommended that these surfaces be
stained, although most surviving examples have long since been painted. For this
house both the window frames and sash were painted bronze green such as Rookwood Shutter Green.

(H. W. Johns Manufacturing Company, *Artistic House Painting*, 1895)

PLATE 64

PLATE 65   This typical clapboard and shingle house of the late nineteenth century is shown in soft browns and yellows with cream trimmings. Note the neo-classical "Venetian Window" in the attic gable. Both the shutters *and* the sash are dark green against the painted clapboards of the first floor and the stained shingles above.   (H. W. Johns Manufacturing Company, *Artistic House Painting*, 1895)

PLATE 66

PLATE 67   By 1895, when this plate was first published, the Colonial Revival style was a rapidly rising tide. The imposing gambrel roof house on its field stone platform is shown in a brownish yellow ("Drab"), trimmed in white with white sash.   (H. W. Johns Manufacturing Company, *Artistic House Painting*, 1895)

PLATE 69   The three colors used here (soft gray body, white trim and sash, cream shutters) are "extensively used on Colonial, Dutch and other styles of houses on this order. The effect may be varied by the use of Buffs, Light Drabs, Creams, etc., for body color, but trimmings and blinds should usually be confined to Cream White or Ivory White."

(H. W. Johns Manufacturing Company, *Artistic House Painting*, 1895)

PLATE 70   On this gambrel roofed house with Neoclassical detailing, the first floor clapboards are painted dark brown with the cedar shingles stained to simulate walnut. The trim is a cream white and the sash reddish brown.

(*Patton Paint Company*, c. 1915)

PLATE 68

72

PLATE 69

PLATE 70

PLATE 71 "A fair example of an old style Colonial dwelling," which "does not admit of much diversity of treatment, but calls for the use of neutral Grays, Buffs, or Light Yellows." The overall trim is white with olive green shutters.
(H. W. Johns Manufacturing Company, *Artistic House Painting*, 1895)

PLATE 72

PLATE 73   This plate illustrates "a modern Colonial house, treated in Yellow body color, White trimmings and Dark Olive Green blinds." Several of the Downing and Renwick yellows might be used here, with the Rookwood or Tiffany olives used on the shutters.

(H. W. Johns Manufacturing Company, *Artistic House Painting*, 1895)

PLATE 74

PLATE 75

PLATE 76

PLATES 76 TO 78 On the eve of World War I, Colonial Revival houses ranged from simple, vernacular boxes with modest "colonial" detailing (Plate 76) to full-blown statements for the comfortable Middle Class (Plate 77). Many of these structures lacked any strong stylistic features (Plate 78); however, they shared a common color palette of grays, yellows, and greens as body colors, usually trimmed in white or ivory. (John W. Masury & Son, c. 1910)

PLATE 75 This Colonial Revival house has been embellished with applied "raised wood carvings" in the gables and along the porch cornice. These elements could be purchased for a few dollars each from the stock of local sash and door companies. The swags shown here on the cornice, for example, were available from the Baltimore Sash and Door Company in 1909 in sections a yard long for $2.25 each. Quite often the swags and wreaths were painted out with the background, occasionally, as here, picked out in the trim color. The temptation to polychrome these minor elements should be resisted. (John W. Masury & Son, c. 1910)

PLATE 78

PLATE 79 "A frame house on a large village lot or country half acre is much more dependent upon paint than the brick or stucco house of the crowded city lot.... A variety of color combinations is permissible on a house of this kind. In general the trimming should be lighter than the house itself. Subdued Green makes an attractive finish for this house if it stands in the open. Dark Grays and Browns are good for body color and will be very durable. The house may also be painted in one color including trim and body, if that color is quite light. In any of these cases the sash should be dark."   (*Lowe Brothers Company*, 1914)

PLATE 80 "White or very light colors should be used for the trim," of this "Down-East" house, "in order to give the appearance of increased size. For the body color Grays are good, or if desired other light colors may be used. Very dark colors rarely look well on a house of this type. If possible the roof should always be stained, particularly if the wing is a single story. When the entire house is two stories this is not so important. Porch floors and the treads of the steps should be of a dark stone or lead color." (*Lowe Brothers Company,* 1914)

PLATE 81 "Repainting the house built years ago is even more general than painting the new house. Styles of building have changed materially in recent years and the painting has changed also. The old house is often dependent largely on the painting to make it attractive as well as to preserve it from decay. The old custom was to use many colors, bringing out the little fancy carvings and scroll work by contrasting colors. Today all these are subdued by using either the body or the trimming color. Where there is much trimming, dark colors are better, at least colors darker than the body. Too great contrasts should be avoided—two shades of the same color, as in the illustration, often giving best results."

(*Lowe Brothers Company*, 1914)

PLATE 82   The gables of this house with exposed "half timbering" are stuccoed with cement tinted brown. The band of shingles is stained reddish yellow and the first floor shingles are stained dark brown. The sash are deep reddish brown, the porch roof light brown, and the floor dark brown.

(*Patton Paint Company*, c. 1915)

PLATE 83   This simple frame house without corner boards is shown in a yellow body with white trim. Note in particular how the bands of the belt course and water table tie the porch to the house. The sash are dark green, the porch floor brown, and the porch ceiling light green.   (*Patton Paint Company*, c. 1915)

PLATE 84   "The plain square house is a popular form for suburban and farm buildings. It is roomy and economical. If properly painted it will be more homelike than many a house of more pretentious architecture." Colors recommended for a house of this type are medium browns and grays, "provided the trimming color is light and gives a good contrast. Lighter colors may be used to good advantage where there is plenty of shrubbery. If the house is where it receives much dust, solid dark colors in Browns may be used. A trimming color of Dark Brown will make the house seem smaller but will give it a solid appearance. The shingles should be stained either Dark Green or Dark Brown."

(*Lowe Brothers Company*, 1914)

PLATE 83

PLATE 84

PLATE 85   A dark green has been used here for the sash of this vernacular house which reflects the influence of Shingle, Colonial Revival, and Bungalow styles. The light trim is particularly effective against the scheme of first floor body color and shingle stain on the second floor and attic gables.

(Patton Paint Company, c. 1915)

PLATE 86   Ionic capitals and a Palladian window provide classical detailing to this otherwise simple house. The body is a reddish yellow which is carried into the shingled gables. The trim is brown and the sash dark green. The porch roof is green and the floor olive.   (*Patton Paint Company*, c. 1915)

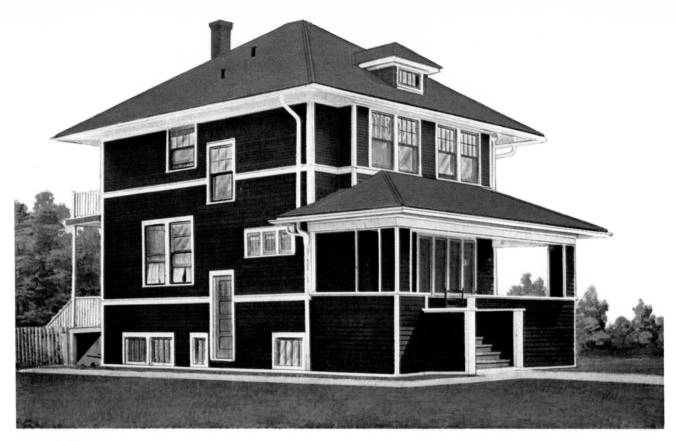

PLATE 87

PLATES 87 AND 88 White used for trim against the darker colors that occasionally carried over into the first decades of this century provides a crisp if
somewhat stark contrast. Plate 88 shows white trim against two colors of stain
on a shingled house. The sash is also white. Plate 87 shows a single body color
(dark brown) and *black* sash which heightens the contrast with the window
frames.   (*Patton Paint Company*, c. 1915)

PLATE 89   "This popular type of suburban house is attractive and practical. As in other forms of present day houses [1914], simplicity in painting is essential— preservation of materials being naturally important. To give the house the appearance of added size, a light first floor and trim should be used, the first story color being continued as trimming color throughout. To give the house solidity . . . dark colors may be used, making the upper story a little darker than the lower. Brown and corresponding dark colors are preferable. Ivory, Cream and Sandstone may be chosen when contrasts and light trimming are desired."

(*Lowe Brothers Company*, 1914)

PLATE 90 "The square house with low roof is probably the most common type of residence building today [1914]. This is due to its economy, both of construction and continued care. Sometimes, as in this illustration, the materials are shingles and wide clapboards; sometimes the upper part is stucco left natural or colored; more frequently the house is all clapboard. When the house is all plain clapboard a greater variety of colors is possible—either light or dark, all one color or with body color and trimming color. Whether light or dark colors are chosen use one color for body, the same or a good harmonious color for trim, and a dark green, black or white for the sash. Do not use many colors. Simplicity in painting is here as important as the style of architecture itself."

(*Lowe Brothers Company*, 1914)

PLATE 91 "The bungalow is distinctively a suburban house, needing grass, shrubbery and trees to make it 'at home.' Its convenience and compactness are important considerations. To make it attractive the colors as well as the architecture must harmonize with the surroundings. White, Grays, soft Greens and Browns will harmonize with nature and give the comfortable, restful feeling that belongs to the bungalow. Either paint or stain may be used in finishing, the latter retaining the weathered idea of the old bungalow which gained its beauty largely by leaving the unprotected lumber to be exposed to the weather.

(*Lowe Brothers Company*, 1914)

PLATE 92 Most paint companies offered darker, warm color schemes for those houses influenced by the Prairie School. Here the body is reddish yellow, or buff, trimmed in brown with dark green sash. The ceiling of the porch is greenish gray, or turquoise, and the floor a darker gray. Note the band of horizontal trim separating the narrow first floor clapboards and the stuccoed second floor.

(*Patton Paint Company*, c. 1915)

PLATE 93 The stucco panels on the second floor of this small house with both Bungalow and Prairie School touches are colored red to pick up the reddish brown of the clapboard first floor. The light buff trim defines the cornice, porch, and water table, and is particularly important in outlining the second floor stucco. Note that the downspouts are painted in the trim color as an extension of the hanging gutters around the cornice. (*Patton Paint Company*, c. 1915)

PLATE 92

PLATE 93

PLATE 94

PLATE 95

92

PLATE 96   The traditional American barn of the late nineteenth century appears here in Rookwood Red, a moderate red brown, trimmed in Rookwood Dark Olive, a grayish olive.

(Sherwin-Williams Paint Company, *Color Applied to Architecture*, 1887)

PLATE 94   "The tendency of modern transportation companies to render their various structures as attractive as possible, and the consequent increase in the demand for technical skill in the accomplishment of this object, induces us to present an illustration of a depot on the Pennsylvania Railroad, the coloring of which is intended to produce a bright and striking effect." Normally, in the 1880s, the first floor of a building would be painted a darker color than the second when a two-color scheme was adopted for the body. Here, however, the colors are reversed, probably to compensate for the shadow cast by the porch roof. Note that the sash color is also lighter than normal to echo the blue and green slate roof.

(Devoe Paint Company, *Exterior Decoration*, 1885)

PLATE 95   The Sherwin-Williams Paint Company was a major supplier of finishes for railroad structures and rolling stock in the 1880s. For this depot they recommended a five color treatment which can be reproduced by painting the first floor, below the windows, Rookwood Dark Green (Trim); the first floor body, Rookwood Jade; the second floor, Rookwood Amber (Trim); the trim, Rookwood Antique Gold; and the sash, Rookwood Red.

(*Catalogue of Paints and Colors for Railway Use*, c. 1885)

PLATE 97 Most authors writing about color in the late nineteenth century recommended that the carriage house, stable, or small barns near the house be painted in a simplified version of the scheme used for the house. Here a small barn is shown in Rookwood Brown, Renwick Golden Oak, and Rookwood Antique Gold. The roof shingles are painted Rookwood Red. An alternative would be the body, Tiffany Olive; the trimming high lights, Renwick Gold; the shadows, Tiffany Moss Green; and the roof, Rookwood Terra Cotta (Trim). Yet another combination might be Rookwood Medium Brown (Trim) on the body; Tiffany Bronze on the trimming high lights; and Rookwood Terra Cotta (Trim) in the shadows.

(Sherwin-Williams Paint Company, *Color Applied to Architecture*, 1888)

PLATE 98 "Frame stable for the better class of city residences." Rookwood Olive, first floor body; Rookwood Terra Cotta (Trim), second floor body; principal trim, Rookwood Amber (Trim); attic gables, Renwick Gold. An alternative scheme might be: Rookwood Medium Brown (Trim), first floor; trim highlights, Renwick Gold, shadows, Tiffany Bronze; gables, carved horse shoe, and upright shingles on second story, Rookwood Red.

(Sherwin-Williams Paint Company, *Color Applied to Architecture*, 1888)

PLATE 99 Another color scheme for the stable illustrated in Plate 98 shows Tiffany Moss Green used on the first floor and for the overall trim. Rookwood Terra Cotta (Trim) appears again on the shingled second story, with Renwick Gold on the recessed panels and in the gables.

(Sherwin-Williams Paint Company, *Color Applied to Architecture*, 1887)

PLATE 98

PLATE 99

95

PLATE 100

PLATE 100   In 1884 The Sherwin-Williams Company published this plate of two commercial buildings, one brick and one frame. "In the smaller cities and towns we frequently see stores of this kind, but the brick ones are seldom painted, and when they are the colors are usually selected without regard to how they will look side by side with buildings adjoining. The question to be considered in making a selection of colors in cases like this is: How will these colors harmonize, either in sympathy or contrast, with those next to them? and unless proper attention is paid to this point, there will be disappointment in the appearance of the store when completed. Perhaps you have seen a store painted that pleased you very much, and you determined to copy it, but somehow it did not look as well as you expected, and you were at a loss to understand why, and it is probably because the colors next to it are not complementary to those you have selected, and detract from their strength and tone. The selections of colors we have made for this plate complement each other and improve the general appearance."

On the brick store front, Sherwin-Williams suggested the use of a dark olive on the posts and panels, and on the remainder the lighter grayish olive; the body of the second and third stories to be moderate reddish brown; the window caps and cornice, the grayish olive; the sash, black, the moldings, dark reddish brown; the sign, gold and black; and the seams, black. On the wooden building next door, the Company suggested that the body of the first floor be painted grayish olive green, the body of the second story, a lighter grayish green, the trim a grayish yellow green, and the sash, dark reddish brown.

Many commercial fronts in the United States dating from the last third of the nineteenth century are brick, but there is little contemporary documentation for painting the trim of these structures. Sherwin-Williams stated, "almost all brick buildings are finished with stone caps and sills; but window and door frames, never being made of stone, should not be painted to represent it. The only part of a brick building that may be painted a stone color is the cornice, because it frequently is made of stone. If the cornice is made of brick, always paint it the same color as the body or main part of the building. All iron work, such as crestings, railings and brackets of balconies, should invariably be painted some dark color, such as black, bronze green or vandyke brown. Sash also should be painted very dark. Black or bronze green are good colors for general work. For olive combinations, a dark rich wine color is good for sash. Vandyke brown is the best general color for sash, as it is a warm color, besides being dark, and it harmonizes perfectly with all warm colors."   (Sherwin-Williams, *House Painting*, 1884)

During the nineteenth century, painting the exterior of a house was more than surface protection, more than presenting a fresh face toward the community. Exterior decoration was a conscious act of beautification in which color was used to enhance the meaning of a building and to delineate its form. From 1820 to 1920, there were six phases marked by gradual shifts in the color palette used for exterior decoration. Colors in vogue during the Neoclassic and Early Victorian periods were light and delicate. Richer, deeper colors evolved in the High and Late Victorian eras. The Edwardian period was characterized by a general lightening of the palette. During the Colonial Revival period, colors became even lighter, and cleaner. In an effort to provide a quick reference for owners of older homes and other preservationists, Heritage Colors™ have been named to reflect and to relate to these six color phases.   *John Crosby Freeman*

CLASSICAL   When Thomas Jefferson symbolically associated old, Roman Republican architectural forms with the new, American Republic, he began the nineteenth-century practice of using historical forms for ideological purposes. Usually painted white with green shutters, Greek Revival buildings (both with and without columns) were the most common type and were pre-fabricated and exported from Boston to the West Coast as early as the 1850s. Classical buildings juxtapose clarity, simplicity, and symmetry to the environment.

DOWNING   Andrew Jackson Downing was a Hudson River Romantic who sought the integration of man with Nature through architecture and landscape. Natural sources, such as sand, earth, clay, straw, and slate, yielded a delicate palette of greys, yellows, tans, and pinks that have remained popular to this day. Downing favored buildings that were varied in outline, Gothic and Italianate in character, and had ornamental brackets, gables, and window caps.

RENWICK   James Renwick was the most successful American-born practitioner of historic revival styles from the 1840s through the 1860s, e.g., Mansardic, High Victorian Gothic, and High Victorian Italianate, this last one probably the most common Victorian building type in America, especially the Middle West. Colors darkened, contrasts were more vivid, and "picking out" of abundant ornamentation became intense; buildings, in short, looked bejeweled.

ROOKWOOD   Maria Longworth Nichols started America's most famous Art Pottery in Cincinnati in 1880. Art Pottery was the most popular expression of The Aesthetic Movement in America. Houses in Aesthetic taste have been called "Queen Anne," "Stick Style," "Eastlake," and "Shingle Style," but all were characterized by using dark browns, olives, oranges, and reds to emphasize architectural materials, mass, volumes, and structure. Reference to historical forms diminishes. Dark colors, used earlier as trim colors, are used as body colors.

TIFFANY   Louis Comfort Tiffany was an interior designer who worked successfully in both the Aesthetic and Art Nouveau styles. Typical houses of this period are products of the related Arts & Crafts Movement, i.e., the Prairie School and the bungalow in which there is little reference to historical forms. Although colors continue to be used to emphasize structure and materials, they are less aggressive and return earlier Victorian shades to prominence, darkened slightly by the Aesthetic experience.

COLONIAL REVIVAL   Early American classical domestic styles become fashionable. Although Colonial Revival features could be found on Aesthetic houses of the 1880s and 1890s, not until the twentieth century did overall classical forms and the delicate coloration associated with them become prominent.

Color Affinity Chart

The color combinations below are based upon color schemes recommended by various nineteenth-century books on exterior decoration. The headings in bold face type are "Heritage Colors"™ and refer to the Sherwin-Williams "Heritage Colors" sample card which has been included with this book. The words in italics are quotations from contemporary sources and general comments about the color. The lists of "Heritage Colors" in roman type below suggest colors for trimming.

 ## THE WHITES

Classical White

Used as an overall body color for Neoclassical and Colonial Revival houses or as a trim color for:

Colonial Revival Blue
Colonial Revival Gray
Colonial Revival Yellow

 ## THE WHITES

Colonial Revival Ivory

Used as an overall body color for Colonial Revival houses, a trim color for some Downing colors or browns in the darker ranges, and as a trim color for:

Colonial Revival Blue
Colonial Revival Gray
Colonial Revival Yellow

 ## THE GRAYS

Downing Sand

"Choicest of all the light semi-neutral tints shown. Its excellence is in the soft tone it possesses, and when a building is completed with this as a body color the effect is peculiarly restful."

Renwick Yellow
Downing Stone
Downing Slate (Trim)
Rookwood Clay
Downing Yellow
Renwick Gold
Rookwood Jade
Tiffany Moss Green
Downing Earth

Downing Stone

"This is one of the best and most popular of the very light neutral tints."

Downing Sand
Downing Slate (Trim)
Downing Straw
Downing Earth
Renwick Rose Beige
Renwick Yellow
Renwick Gold
Rookwood Clay
Rookwood Antique Gold
Tiffany Moss Green

 ## THE GRAYS

Downing Slate (Trim)

Never a body color.

Renwick Heather (Trim)

Never a body color.

Rookwood Clay

A color "extensively used. It is neither very light nor very dark; it is clear, not too positive; indeed, it is almost neutral, and looks well on a large variety of structures." For porch ceilings and fancy gables Renwick Yellow, Renwick Gold, and Downing Yellow were popular.

Rookwood Dark Brown (Trim)
Downing Slate (Trim)
Downing Earth
Downing Stone
Rookwood Antique Gold
Renwick Golden Oak
Renwick Gold

Colonial Revival Gray

Colonial Revival Ivory
Classical White

Color Affinity Chart

The color combinations below are based upon color schemes recommended by various nineteenth-century books on exterior decoration. The headings in bold face type are "Heritage Colors"™ and refer to the Sherwin-Williams "Heritage Colors" sample card which has been included with this book. The words in italics are quotations from contemporary sources and general comments about the color. The lists of "Heritage Colors" in roman type below suggest colors for trimming.

 THE YELLOWS

Downing Yellow

Downing Sand
Downing Stone

Downing Cream

Downing Stone
Downing Slate (Trim)
Downing Earth
Renwick Heather (Trim)
Rookwood Antique Gold

Renwick Yellow

"This tint is often used with good effect, but it is subject to some of the same objections we have to white; it is rather too glaring or bright." This color may also require several coats to cover a dark surface.

Downing Sand
Renwick Heather (Trim)
Downing Stone
Rookwood Clay
Downing Earth
Rookwood Antique Gold
Rookwood Jade
Downing Slate (Trim)
Tiffany Moss Green

Renwick Gold

"This is a beautiful light buff, much used, and with most satisfactory results."

Downing Sand
Downing Stone
Rookwood Jade
Downing Yellow
Tiffany Moss Green

THE YELLOWS

Rookwood Antique Gold

"This is one of the tints which the ladies call 'perfectly lovely.' As a body color it may be trimmed with any yellowish tint of the softest effect, and will also harmonize with other not too positive tints and shades."

Renwick Yellow
Renwick Gold
Downing Yellow
Downing Stone
Rookwood Clay
Rookwood Jade
Rookwood Dark Brown (Trim)

Tiffany Bronze

Rookwood Dark Green (Trim)
Rookwood Dark Olive
Renwick Rose Beige
Rookwood Red
Rookwood Olive

Colonial Revival Yellow

Colonial Revival Ivory
Classical White

THE BLUES

Colonial Revival Blue

Never used as a trim color.

Classical White
Colonial Revival Ivory

Color Affinity Chart

The color combinations below are based upon color schemes recommended by various nineteenth-century books on exterior decoration. The headings in bold face type are "Heritage Colors"™ and refer to the Sherwin-Williams "Heritage Colors" sample card which has been included with this book. The words in italics are quotations from contemporary sources and general comments about the color. The lists of "Heritage Colors" in roman type below suggest colors for trimming.

 ## THE BROWNS

Downing Straw

Downing Earth
Downing Stone
Downing Slate (Trim)
Renwick Rose Beige
Rookwood Medium Brown (Trim)

Downing Earth

"One of the choicest of the semi-neutral shades ... there is a peculiar softness and beauty to it not easily explained, but universally admired."

Downing Straw
Downing Stone
Rookwood Dark Brown (Trim)
Rookwood Clay
Downing Slate (Trim)
Renwick Golden Oak
Renwick Rose Beige
Rookwood Blue Green
Rookwood Jade

Renwick Beige

Renwick Heather (Trim)
Downing Stone
Downing Slate (Trim)
Renwick Gold
Rookwood Dark Brown (Trim)

Renwick Rose Beige

"This clear, bright, semi-neutral tint is quite a favorite as a body color. Being in good contrast with foliage and lawn surroundings, therefore the 'complementary' effect is a pleasing surprise .... This is best with no other color, except foundations, roofs, steps, and sash."

Tiffany Bronze
Tiffany Moss Green
Tiffany Olive
Rookwood Blue Green
Rookwood Jade
Downing Straw

 ## THE BROWNS

Renwick Golden Oak

A "delicate soft brown" that mixes well with all other browns. Use yellows and reds for gables, porch ceilings, sash, and shutters.

Rookwood Brown
Rookwood Medium Brown (Trim)

Rookwood Brown

"This is one of the fine browns which have come into use again [1887], and admits of combination with other soft colors to produce a most pleasing effect; it also looks well in contrast with the olives."

Renwick Golden Oak
Rookwood Medium Brown (Trim)
Rookwood Olive
Rookwood Dark Olive
Tiffany Moss Green
Tiffany Olive
Renwick Olive

Rookwood Medium Brown (Trim)

Often used in combination with other browns. "When these browns are used together care should be taken to avoid both 'top-heavy' and 'flat' effects by placing the darkest color below a good contrasting one."

Rookwood Dark Red (Trim)
Rookwood Brown
Renwick Golden Oak

Rookwood Dark Brown (Trim)

"A very good color, but not quite so largely used as a body color as before the introduction of more positive shades."

Rookwood Clay
Downing Earth
Tiffany Olive
Rookwood Antique Gold
Renwick Rose Beige
Rookwood Terra Cotta (Trim)

Color Affinity Chart

The color combinations below are based upon color schemes recommended by various nineteenth-century books on exterior decoration. The headings in bold face type are "Heritage Colors"™ and refer to the Sherwin-Williams "Heritage Colors" sample card which has been included with this book. The words in italics are quotations from contemporary sources and general comments about the color. The lists of "Heritage Colors" in roman type below suggest colors for trimming.

 ## THE GREENS

Renwick Fence Green

Always used as a trim color; may be used in place of the Rookwood trim greens.

Rookwood Jade

"A very fashionable tint."

Rookwood Blue Green
Rookwood Dark Green (Trim)
Downing Sand
Downing Earth
Rookwood Antique Gold
Renwick Rose Beige
Renwick Yellow

Rookwood Blue Green

"Even more desirable than [Rookwood Jade], because it admits of more positive trimmings."

Rookwood Dark Green (Trim)
Rookwood Olive
Rookwood Terra Cotta (Trim)
Rookwood Red
Rookwood Jade
Downing Earth
Downing Stone

Rookwood Dark Green (Trim)

Rarely used as an overall body color.

Rookwood Dark Red (Trim)
Rookwood Red
Rookwood Olive
Rookwood Terra Cotta (Trim)
Tiffany Olive
Tiffany Bronze
Rookwood Olive
Rookwood Amber (Trim)

 ## THE GREENS

Rookwood Sash Green

Always used with other trim colors and never as a body color.

Rookwood Olive
Rookwood Shutter Green
Rookwood Red
Rookwood Amber (Trim)

Rookwood Shutter Green

Always used with other trim colors and never as a body color.

Rookwood Sash Green
Rookwood Amber (Trim)
Rookwood Dark Olive
Rookwood Olive
Rookwood Dark Green (Trim)
Rookwood Dark Brown (Trim)

Tiffany Palm Green

Rookwood Olive
Rookwood Red
Rookwood Medium Brown (Trim)

Tiffany Moss Green

Renwick Rose Beige
Downing Sand
Renwick Gold
Downing Stone
Renwick Yellow

Color Affinity Chart

The color combinations below are based upon color schemes recommended by various nineteenth-century books on exterior decoration. The headings in bold face type are "Heritage Colors"™ and refer to the Sherwin-Williams "Heritage Colors" sample card which has been included with this book. The words in italics are quotations from contemporary sources and general comments about the color. The lists of "Heritage Colors" in roman type below suggest colors for trimming.

 ## THE OLIVES

Renwick Olive

Used in combination with other olives or in place of Tiffany Olive when a clearer olive is needed.

Rookwood Olive

"This is a . . . desirable color, destined to be used more and more as people overcome their prejudice to new positive colors."

Rookwood Dark Red (Trim)
Rookwood Red
Rookwood Dark Green (Trim)
Rookwood Dark Olive
Downing Slate (Trim)
Rookwood Terra Cotta (Trim)
Tiffany Olive
Tiffany Bronze
Rookwood Amber (Trim)

 ## THE OLIVES

Rookwood Dark Olive

"This is one of the most popular dark shades for house painting." (1887)

Rookwood Red
Rookwood Dark Red (Trim)
Rookwood Terra Cotta (Trim)
Rookwood Olive
Tiffany Olive
Tiffany Bronze
Rookwood Amber (Trim)

Tiffany Olive

Rookwood Dark Green (Trim)
Rookwood Dark Olive
Renwick Rose Beige
Rookwood Dark Brown (Trim)
Rookwood Red
Rookwood Olive
Rookwood Dark Red (Trim)

 ## THE REDS

Rookwood Red

"This is, in all respects, an excellent red for the body of a house, inasmuch as it does not fade or change as much as most other reds, and is neither too bright nor too dull. Olives and greens contrast best for trimmings."

Rookwood Dark Olive
Rookwood Dark Green (Trim)
Tiffany Olive
Rookwood Olive
Rookwood Amber (Trim)
Tiffany Bronze

 ## THE REDS

Rookwood Dark Red (Trim)

"This, while one of the richest house colors ever produced, is too dark to be generally used for the entire body of a house. It is quite suitable, and is largely used on the first or lower story of buildings having a belting course to separate the stories." Also often used for doors and sash.

Rookwood Dark Olive
Rookwood Dark Green (Trim)
Rookwood Olive
Tiffany Olive
Rookwood Medium Brown (Trim)

 ## THE ORANGES

Rookwood Amber (Trim)

"This is not generally used as a body color for the plain class of buildings where the entire body is of one color, but is very useful in the modern Queen Anne and Swiss structures for second story, gables or roofs, when other colors are in good contrast."

Rookwood Medium Brown (Trim)
Rookwood Brown
Rookwood Red
Rookwood Terra Cotta (Trim)

 ## THE ORANGES

Rookwood Terra Cotta (Trim)

"This is most useful as a contrasting color in gables, second stories, etc."

Rookwood Amber (Trim)
Rookwood Blue Green
Rookwood Dark Green (Trim)
Rookwood Dark Olive
Renwick Golden Oak

CORNICE

4. Edge of crown mold
5. Crown
6. Fasciae
7. Bed mold
8. Dentals
9. Frieze
10. Panel mold
11. Panel
12. Architrave
13. Sunk face of bracket
14. Raised face of bracket
15. Bracket panel
16. Bracket margin
17. Soffit

26. CORNER BOARD

WATER TABLE

28. Slope
29. Edge
30. Face

WINDOW

32. Face	38. Sill
33. Cap fillet	39 Apron
34. Cap mold	40. Reveal
35. Cap panel	41. Edge
36. Keystone	51. Sash
37. Chamfer	52. Transom

DOOR

54. Stiles and rails
55. Mold
56. Projecting part of panel
57. Receding part of panel

BLINDS

58. Slats
59. Frame

PORCH

60. Balustrade post
61. Balustrade base
62. Balustrade rail
63. Receding part of baluster
64. Projecting part of baluster
65. Abacus
66. Capital
67. Neck mold
68. Chamfer
69. Shaft
70. Rosette
71. Plinth
72. Plinth mold
73. Rail
74. Dado
75. Dado panel
76. Base
77. Base mold
78. Ornamental rail
79. Ornamental panel
80. Ornamental chamfer
81. Bead below steps
82. Panel mold below steps
83. Panel below steps

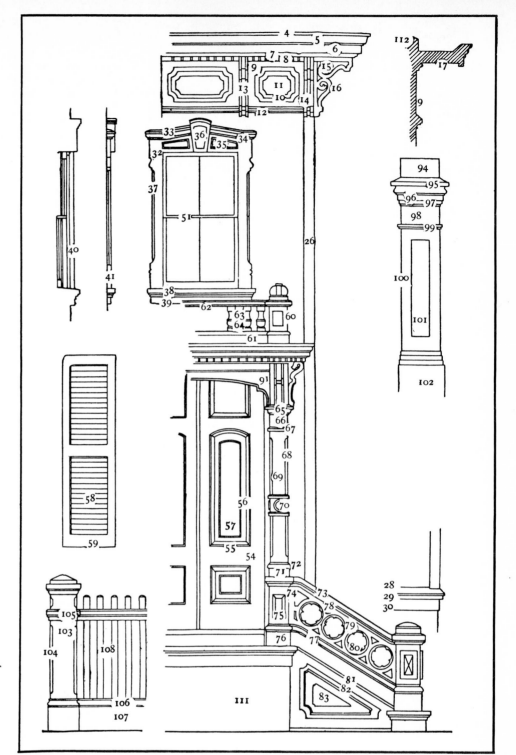

CHIMNEY

94. Top of cap
95. Crown mold of cap
96. Faciae of cap
97. Bed mold of cap
98. Frieze of cap
99. Architrave
100. Shaft
101. Panels
102. Base

FENCE

103. Post
104. Post chamfer
105. Upper rail
106. Lower rail
107. Base
108. Pickets

111. FOUNDATION

112. ROOF

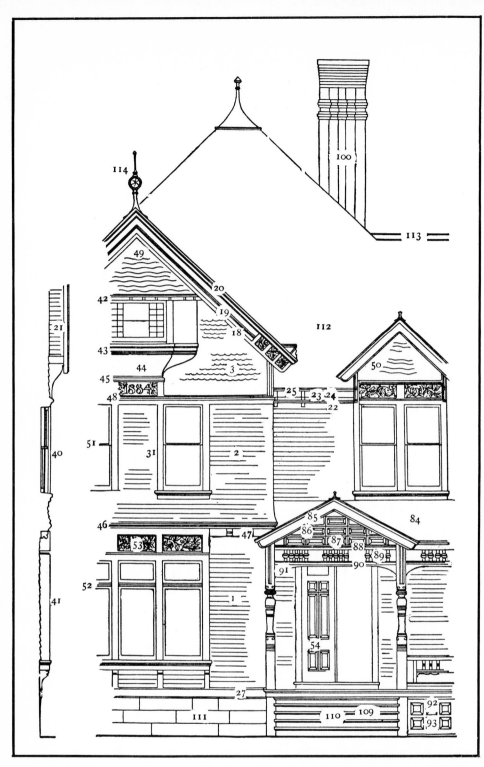

BODY

1. *First story*
2. *Second story*
3. *Attic*

CORNICE

18.–20. Bargeboard
18. *Face rafter margin*
19. *Face rafter mold*
20. *Eaves mold*
21. *Ceiling under eaves*
23. *Gutter face*
24. *Gutter brackets*
25. *Gutter cap*

27. WATER TABLE

WINDOW FRAME

40. *Reveal*
41. *Edge*

ATTIC WINDOW

42. *Cornice*
43. *Sill mold*
44. *Cove*
45. *Base mold*

46. BELT COURSE

47. BEAM ENDS

48. MOLD UNDER ATTIC

49. GABLE OVER ATTIC WINDOW

50. DORMER GABLE

51. WINDOW SASH

52. WINDOW TRANSOM

DOOR

54. *Stiles and rails*

PORCH

84. *Roof*
85. *Face rafter*
86. *Gable rail*
87. *Gable panels*
88. *Plate*
89. *Cornice balusters*
90. *Cornice rail*
91. *Cornice curve or bracket*
92. *Rails below*
93. *Panels below*

CHIMNEY

100. *Shaft*

STEPS

109. *Tread mold*
110. *Riser*

111. FOUNDATION

ROOF

113. *Ridge roll*
114. *Iron finials*

Architectural Glossary

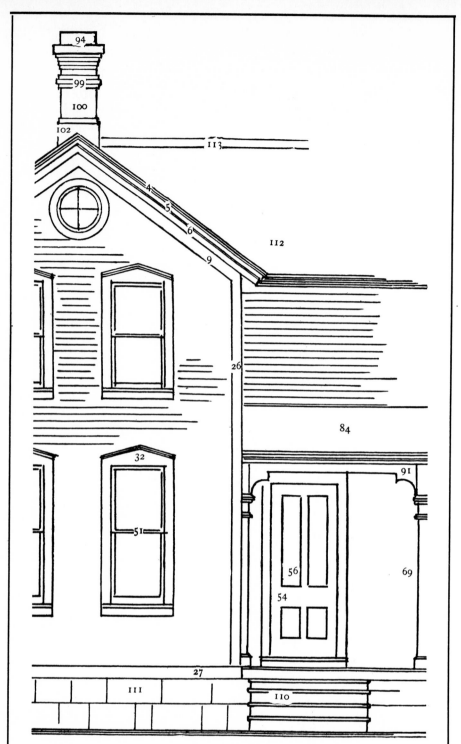

CORNICE

4. *Edge of crown mold*
5. *Crown*
6. *Fasciae*
9. *Frieze*

26. CORNER BOARD

27. WATER TABLE

WINDOW

32. *Face*
51. *Sash*

DOOR

54. *Stiles and rails*
56. *Receding part of panel*

PORCH

69. *Shaft*
84. *Roof*
91. *Cornice curve or bracket*

CHIMNEY

94. *Top of cap*
99. *Architrave*
100. *Shaft*
102. *Base*

110. STEP RISER

111. FOUNDATION

ROOF

113. *Ridge roll*

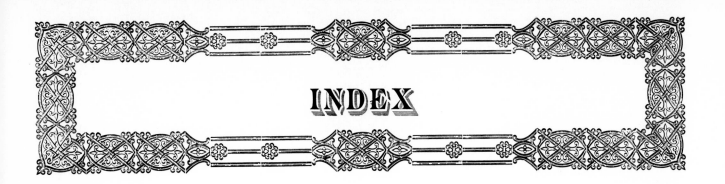

INDEX

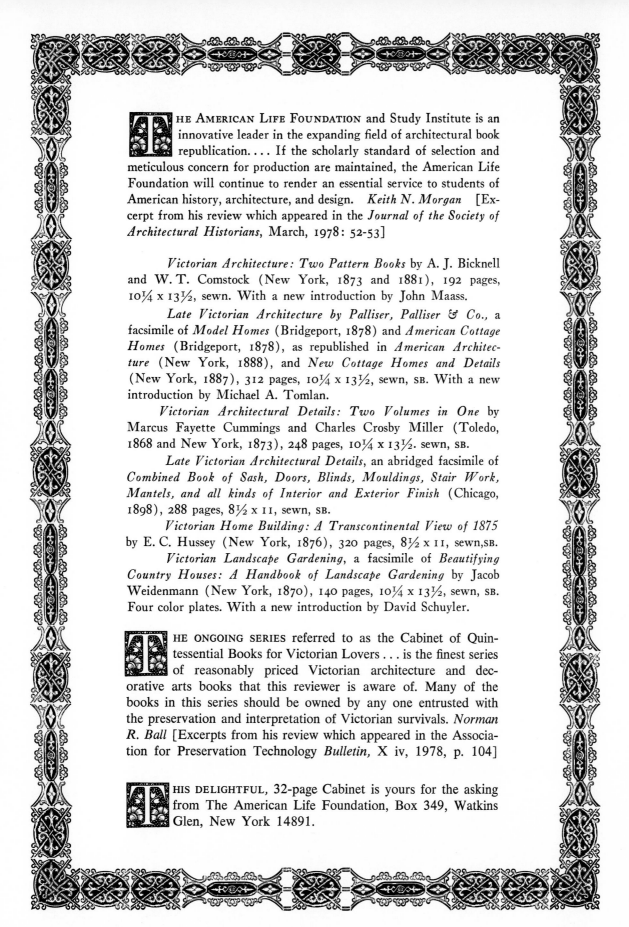

THE AMERICAN LIFE FOUNDATION and Study Institute is an innovative leader in the expanding field of architectural book republication. ... If the scholarly standard of selection and meticulous concern for production are maintained, the American Life Foundation will continue to render an essential service to students of American history, architecture, and design. *Keith N. Morgan* [Excerpt from his review which appeared in the *Journal of the Society of Architectural Historians*, March, 1978: 52-53]

Victorian Architecture: Two Pattern Books by A. J. Bicknell and W. T. Comstock (New York, 1873 and 1881), 192 pages, 10¼ x 13½, sewn. With a new introduction by John Maass.

Late Victorian Architecture by Palliser, Palliser & Co., a facsimile of *Model Homes* (Bridgeport, 1878) and *American Cottage Homes* (Bridgeport, 1878), as republished in *American Architecture* (New York, 1888), and *New Cottage Homes and Details* (New York, 1887), 312 pages, 10¼ x 13½, sewn, SB. With a new introduction by Michael A. Tomlan.

Victorian Architectural Details: Two Volumes in One by Marcus Fayette Cummings and Charles Crosby Miller (Toledo, 1868 and New York, 1873), 248 pages, 10¼ x 13½. sewn, SB.

Late Victorian Architectural Details, an abridged facsimile of *Combined Book of Sash, Doors, Blinds, Mouldings, Stair Work, Mantels, and all kinds of Interior and Exterior Finish* (Chicago, 1898), 288 pages, 8½ x 11, sewn, SB.

Victorian Home Building: A Transcontinental View of 1875 by E. C. Hussey (New York, 1876), 320 pages, 8½ x 11, sewn, SB.

Victorian Landscape Gardening, a facsimile of *Beautifying Country Houses: A Handbook of Landscape Gardening* by Jacob Weidenmann (New York, 1870), 140 pages, 10¼ x 13½, sewn, SB. Four color plates. With a new introduction by David Schuyler.

THE ONGOING SERIES referred to as the Cabinet of Quintessential Books for Victorian Lovers ... is the finest series of reasonably priced Victorian architecture and decorative arts books that this reviewer is aware of. Many of the books in this series should be owned by any one entrusted with the preservation and interpretation of Victorian survivals. *Norman R. Ball* [Excerpts from his review which appeared in the Association for Preservation Technology *Bulletin,* X iv, 1978, p. 104]

THIS DELIGHTFUL, 32-page Cabinet is yours for the asking from The American Life Foundation, Box 349, Watkins Glen, New York 14891.

CENTURY OF COLOR was designed and produced by Walnut Grove Design, Watkins Glen, NY. Color separations were provided by Callahan Color Service, Binghamton, NY. Composition was provided by Tier Oldstyle Typesetting Company, Binghamton, NY. Preparation, printing, and binding was provided by Valley Offset, Inc., Deposit, NY.

Papers used are seventy-pound Mead Moistrite Matte Web for color plates, seventy-pound Champion Panaprint Web for text, and ten-point Carolina coated one side for the softcover portion of the edition. Body type is Linotype Century Expanded. Display types are Ultra Bodoni, Latin Wide, Clarendon, and Aquatint. The Minionette Chromatic Border and the initials are from the Victorian Typographical Collections of The American Life Foundation.

This edition consists of 40,000 copies of which 30,000 are softcover and 10,000 are casebound. The Sherwin-Williams Company subscribed to half of the edition. The Old-House Journal Corp. subscribed to 5,000 softcover copies.

HERITAGE COLORS™ color card, supplied courtesy The Sherwin-Williams Company, was supervised by Chris Wearsch, Director of Color and Design. Designed by Pitt Studios, Cleveland, OH, it was printed on eighty-pound Cameo Cover Dull by The Sherwin-Williams Graphic Arts Unit, Cleveland, OH, who also color-chipped the forty "Heritage Colors" in SWP® Gloss House and Trim Paint (Oil Base).

$10.00

This is a detail of a front porch bracket from the Queen Victoria Inn, shown on the front cover. Offering "Bed & Breakfast Victorian Style" at 102 Ocean Street, Cape May, NJ 08204, the Queen Victoria Inn is the first building painted in Heritage Colors™ in accordance with the principles presented in this book, *Century of Color*. Owned by Joan Wells, former Executive Director of The Victorian Society in America, and her husband Dane, the Queen Victoria Inn, built in 1881, is enjoying a centennial along with The Sherwin-Williams Company who contributed the following Heritage Colors to this preservation project: Rookwood Blue Green for the body, Rookwood Dark Green for the trim, Rookwood Red for the roof, and Rookwood Dark Red for the sash.

CENTURY OF COLOR, 1820-1920

CENTURY OF COLOR, 1820–1920 is a documentary history of American exterior decoration in 100 plates taken from the collections of The Athenaeum of Philadelphia and the archives of The Sherwin-Williams Company. It is a practical guide, helping old house owners and other preservationists in the selection and placement of exterior coloration. The publication of *Century of Color* coincides with the introduction of a new line of forty, authentic, "Heritage Colors" by The Sherwin-Williams Company in the centennial year of Sherwin-Williams Paint. Displayed in forty, large, sample chips on a fold-out color card that can be studied while reading this book, these "Heritage Colors" have been selected from documentary sources by Dr. Roger W. Moss, author of *Century of Color* and executive director of The Athenaeum of Philadelphia. In addition to the 100 beautiful plates and handsome color card, *Century of Color* also features: an extensive essay on exterior decoration; a Victorian architectural glossary; a microscopic analysis and Munsell notation of fifty-seven colors found on two of the earliest color cards to survive; a bibliography of published sources; and a "color affinity chart" keyed to the forty, authenticated "Heritage Colors."

ROGER MOSS is shown here suggesting colors for the Queen Victoria Inn on the front cover. Dr. Moss, a historian, is a native of Ohio. Since 1968 he has been the Executive Director of The Athenaeum of Philadelphia, an independent research library founded in 1814 which specializes in nineteenth-century social and cultural history. He is an officer of The Victorian Society in America, a director of the Historic House Association of America and of several historic houses, most notably Harriton, home of Charles Thomson, Secretary of the Continental Congress, and Cliveden, a property of the National Trust for Historic Preservation. He has lectured on painting the historic house to audiences in all parts of the country. In his foreword, the author writes, "it is hoped that this book will encourage the owners of American houses built in the last century to select colors that are historically proper for the age of the structure and to place those colors to emphasize correctly the rich character and detailing intended by the original builders."

T3-BHW-404

ISBN: 0-89257-051-2